Climbing From
the Fifth Station

Climbing From the Fifth Station

A guide to building teams that work!

George A. Ebert

Writers Club Press
San Jose New York Lincoln Shanghai

Climbing From the Fifth Station
A guide to building teams that work!

All Rights Reserved © 2001 by George A. Ebert

Writers Club Press
an imprint of iUniverse.com, Inc.

For information address:
iUniverse.com, Inc.
5220 S 16th, Ste. 200
Lincoln, NE 68512
www.iuniverse.com

ISBN: 0-595-18185-6

Printed in the United States of America

To Patsy—who never stopped believing.

Epigraph

Training is everything. The peach was once a bitter almond; cauliflower is nothing but Cabbage with a College Education.

Mark Twain

The Tragedy of Pudd'nhead Wilson and the Comedy of the Extraordinary Twins

CONTENTS

A RULE AND THREE PRINCIPLES

I climbed Mt. Fuji in the summer of 1978. At the time I was stationed at Yokota Air Base, just outside Tokyo. Climbing Mt. Fuji was one of the things one *did*. The general plan called for a late afternoon start and an easy climb to the summit before dawn. The prize was watching the sunrise over Japan from this highest and most sacred point. Following a glorious sunrise, the descent down a lava slide was quick and a hot lunch back at the base a comfortable expectation.

Needless to say, the plan didn't work out as expected. It took longer, required more work, cost more and produced something less than the spectacular results promised. It proved, however, to be a liminal experience for me. Over the course of the years I have returned time and again to the lessons of Fuji. They've given me inspiration, enlightenment and a field guide for practical living. It is that sense that frames this work—enlightened practicality. *Climbing From the Fifth Station* is very much about obtaining peak experiences through direct, practical approaches. It's about simple, straightforward action. But it's also about *enlightened* simplicity and action. It draws on what we *know to be true* to shape our current journey.

Climbing From the Fifth Station is written to help teams become successful. The principles work for all teams—office teams, social teams, sports teams, families and even couples. The principles are dynamic. They challenge you to simultaneously look within—at how you respond to events—and without—at how you initiate actions involving others. As an individual, they provide a means of interpreting your experience in a way that maximizes positive results. As a team player, they provide a structure

1

in which you can foster and benefit from the success of others. As a team leader, they demonstrate how to synergize the efforts of those on your team. The principles are intuitive, although they should be self-consciously applied. They are easy to use because they just make sense!

The Fuji Rule

Ten stations mark the trail to Mt. Fuji's summit. These stations are stopping points where rest, refreshment and opportunities for reflection are available. My climb began at the first station. It was a magnificent shrine under a sun light mottled canopy of evergreen and cedar. Incense wafted through the air and a clear spring bubbled nearby. Far, far in the distance loomed the summit of Fuji. It was apparent the climb to the peak would take several days—not the several hours we had allotted—and would require serious hiking and camping gear. Interrupting my reflection, I retraced my steps, boarded a bus and rode to the fifth station.

Virtually everyone, it turned out, begins climbing from the fifth station. For most visitors to Mt. Fuji, this is as far as they get. The view is great, the photo opportunities impressive and the sense of "having been there," indisputable.

Also indisputable, is the fact that by climbing from the fifth station, your chances of reaching the summit by dawn are a near certainty. This is the first lesson that Fuji yields. In life, as on Fuji, climbing begins from the fifth station. This means that in any given situation, everyone begins with most of what they will need to succeed. Everyone joining a team or entering into a relationship already possesses most of the skills required to fully accomplish their goal.

The beautiful symmetry of Mt. Fuji helps demonstrate this point. Owing to its volcanic origins, Fuji forms an almost perfect cone. The distance from the base to the summit is 3,650 meters. The halfway point or fifth station is roughly 1,825 meters, an equal distance from either the base or summit. Now consider the *volume* of Fuji. By the time you arrive at the fifth station, fully 90% of the mountain's volume is beneath you. Thus at the halfway point of your climb, you've mastered 90% of the challenge with a meager 10% left to go. You're standing on a massive base—a *foundation* of stone—that will support your climb to the peak.

If we think of *distance* in this example as the goal and *volume* as cumulative life experience, it's easy to see that you start any challenge from your personal fifth station. That is, you always begin from the bedrock foundation of your experience, education and training. That foundation reflects the 90% of what is required to succeed. Too often people assume that they're "coming up from nowhere," or "starting at square one," when in fact they are richly endowed with resources. Granted, the new challenge may require that old skills are refined or new ones developed, but they are always built upon a massive personal foundation.

The members of every team and the partners in every relationship begin their journeys with a wealth of resources to apply to the job at hand. To climb from the fifth station is to recognize and mobilize the abundant resources that are immediately available. Understanding this abundance is the beginning of confidence, and confidence, as we shall see, *is* the fifth station.

This is the Fuji Rule. No matter what the task or challenge, we should always begin with our *foundation*—with what we *know*. We should build on our *strengths* and *assets*. Rather than obsessing over areas for improvement, we should leverage *what we're doing right*.

Three Principles

Principles are truths, laws or assumptions. They express the rules that underlie a specific process. There are three principles that underlie *Fifth Station* team building. Together they provide the structure of everything else that will follow. They also provide a quick check on all actions associated with the team. They can be used as an initial filter or criteria for decision-making. If the action measures up, you're on the right path. If it doesn't, you'll know where to begin revisions. As with everything else at the Fifth Station, these principles are intuitively applicable. They'll help you discern what's *really* going on, avoid extremism, and eliminate complexity. It all begins with WYSINWYG.

The First Principle: WYSINWYG

In early 1973, Butler Lampson, Chuck Thacker and a team of other engineers working at Xerox Corporation's Palo Alto Research Center, or PARC, completed the first personal computer prototype. They dubbed the machine *Alto*. Alto's graphics were one of its most extraordinary features. Prior to Alto, all computer screens were calligraphic. When a user keyed a letter, a code was generated that triggered phosphors on the screen to paint the letter. Though an efficient mechanism, the result was a display vastly inferior to any print medium. Alto resolved the problem through bit mapping. With this system, every pixel on the screen was mapped to a single bit in the computer's memory. With bit mapping, the computer understood everything on the screen as a graphic. Pictures, charts, graphs or individual letters were all understood as graphics. Though requiring huge amounts of memory, the results were startling. For the first time, what you saw on the screen was what you would see with high quality printing. This amazing feature came to be called *WYSIWYG—what you see is what you get.*

Though revolutionary in almost every way, almost a hundred years prior to Alto, another transforming technology introduced an almost identical concept. The technology was photography and the advancement was the single lens reflex camera. A single lens reflex—or SLR—camera enables the photographer to frame and focus through the lens rather than through a separate viewfinder. By looking through the lens, the photographer is able to see precisely what will be captured on the film. Almost everyone is familiar with the point-and-shoot alternative, which is responsible for the recording of so many thumbs, camera straps and lopped off heads found in family photo albums. After a hundred years, SLR is still the standard because it gives the photographer precise control of the medium.

SLR and WYSIWYG are technological manifestations of man's deep desire to know what's going on. The product of knowing what's going on is *control*. If you have an accurate sense of what's happening, you can control yourself, others, the environment and events. This knowledge provides security and to some extent, confidence. We can find indications of the desire all around us, from Joe Friday trying to make the case with, "just the facts," to the technical analysis of the stock market. People strive for the knowledge that will help them to control their lives.

The desire to *know* implies that we *can* know. That we can master and own a subject. By improving our technologies and amassing facts, we can determine, with certainty, all the dimensions of a situation. More importantly, it implies that there is an end point from which further exploration is unnecessary. The assumption is that the number of facts in any situation is finite. When we have collected all the facts, we will have complete knowledge. It is an approach that seeks to drive out uncertainty, minimize risk and eliminate surprise. *And that is why it is dangerous.*

The *Fifth Station's* first principle is that no matter what the relationship, situation or event, *what you see is **never** what you get—WYSINWYG.* This is a powerful concept, for it suggests that you will never fully know what is going on. No matter how new your software, how fast your computer, how good your analysis or how frequent your focus groups, you will always operate on partial information. Every decision will, of necessity, involve some degree of uncertainty. An individual or organization is at greatest risk when it ignores this and loses its capacity for surprise.

Though our desire to know what is going on is powerful, the expectation that we *can* is largely counterintuitive. It's axiomatic that appearances are deceiving. Take for a moment the mystery genre. Whether literary, cinematic or video, mysteries provide phenomenally popular entertainment. Yet despite their enduring appeal, the plots are strictly formula. A crime is committed, initial facts suggest one solution, but careful sleuthing produces a surprise ending. Thus, the initial premise of almost every mystery is WYSINWYG. That they remain popular under-scores their intuitive appeal. We like to be surprised and we expect our world to be more than what it appears to be.

Not surprisingly, WYSINWYG is a central theme of the Christian gospels. All four gospels try to make the case that the carpenter's kid is something more. From birth to Emmaus, people see a Jewish, Mediterranean peasant. Who would have guessed that he would trans-form civilization? A great deal of the joy Christians find in the gospels is rooted in the surprise and amazement wrought by Jesus. From wine into water, to healing, to meager foodstuffs feeding thousands, WYSINWYG proved electrifying to the crowds.

WYSINWYG is active on the battlefield as well. It's a common military strategy and included in two of the principles of war. A commander using the principles recognizes that what he sees of the enemy is never a com-plete picture. By remaining open to the possibility of surprise, he satisfies the seventh principle of war, *security*, which states that the enemy should never be permitted to gain an unexpected advantage. WYSINWYG is also active in the eighth principle, *surprise*, which requires the commander to strike the enemy in a time, place or manner for which he is unprepared. In essence, he places himself in the other commander's shoes and synchro-nizes what will appear to the enemy as improbable.

The true power of WYSINWYG is that there is always something more going on. There is always something just out of site that will transform the routine into the wonderful. WYSINWYG requires that you never lose touch with your capacity for surprise and remain vigilant for opportunity. It doesn't ask for a Pollyanna naiveté, or suggest that unpleasant surprises not be actively avoided. Rather, WYSINWYG suggests that you will be better able to avoid negatives if you maintain a positive state of anticipation.

Leaders, who confidently declare that they have "seen it all," have lost more than their capacity for surprise. They have actually lost the ability to anticipate change and prepare for it. Ironically, accepting that you won't ever "know it all" restores the *control* behind the initial desire to know it all.

Of course, WYSINWYG is at the very heart of the *Fifth Station*. The ability not only to anticipate surprise, but also to actually expect the unexpected will open you to opportunities and insights otherwise unavailable. The premise of *Fifth Station* thinking is that *you are almost there already*. WYSINWYG reminds you to find the hidden skills, strengths and resources available to you *now*. The first principle advises you to always, *take a second look*.

The Second Principle: Balance

In a warm, nurturing rain and under delicately blooming trees, Prince Siddartha was born to King Suddhadana and Queen Maya in 560 B. C. E. The birth was attended by many natural miracles and the child himself was marked in such a way that two opposing prophesies were made about his future. One prophecy foretold greatness as a king, the other, life as a homeless monk.

Recognizing his son's vast potential, King Suddhadana raised Siddartha in an atmosphere of total luxury. He never knew want, or pain, or sorrow. His world was an ideal fantasy in which illness and death were unknown. He knew only happiness and believed that no other state of being existed. Siddartha's joy escalated when he married a beautiful princess and they had a robust son. All was perfection in Siddartha's universe.

But Prince Siddartha became restless. Despite his father's efforts to shield him, at age 29 Siddartha left the palace and confronted the world. As he journeyed, he first met an old man. He was shocked to see a man in such a condition because the Prince knew nothing of aging. He then encountered a sick man and was deeply saddened by his first glimpse of human suffering. He finally saw a corpse and was muted by his first encounter with death. As he brooded on these revelations, he saw a monk, begging, in a yellow robe. As he faced the reality of decay, pain and death, he determined, like the monk, to do something about it.

Renouncing the world, as he had known it, Siddartha began his journey for enlightenment. Dissatisfied with his first teachers, Siddartha spent six years in meditation while living as an extreme ascetic. Denying himself almost all food, he often ate as little as one seed a day. After years of self-mortification he resembled a living skeleton. Though enlightenment evaded him, weakness began to gradually overtake him.

One day Siddartha heard the singing of young girls in the distance. As they grew closer he heard the words of their song;

> The tune of the sitar makes dancing light,
> So tune not in the depths, nor in the heights.
> Too taut—the string breaks
> And cannot sing.
> Too slack—it is mute
>   And will not sing.
> So tune the sitar
> Not in the depths, nor in the heights.

As the voices faded away, Siddartha found wisdom in the song. He recognized that enlightenment could not be found in the extremes of indolence or asceticism, or being and non-being. That truth was not at the edge, but in the middle. He then knew that enlightenment was to be found on the middle path. It was here that insight would lead to tranquility, wisdom and nirvana. And it is this insight that becomes the second principle of the Fifth Station.

The second principle is that people and organizations are most effective when operating with equilibrium or *balance*. That is, the best strategies, approaches and decisions will be made, not at the fringes of rationality or emotion, but in a well-orchestrated balance of all factors. Success will be found in the middle. Problems develop when people or organizations operate at the extremes. The results can be disastrous as when the management technique du jour is heavy-handed in defiance of a healthy corporate culture, or when growth is pursued without constraint, or new technologies supplant the old before staffs are fully trained. The backlash can be as varied as abandonment of potentially good ideas, to customer dissatisfaction, to out- and-out bankruptcy.

Zeal for extremes is common, though counterintuitive. Whether it involves the race to embrace the new, or undying devotion to the past, nothing is ever maintained at the extremes. In time, often a dizzyingly short time, the fury and fantasy evaporates. Things correct themselves. Balance is restored.

The power of balance should not be underestimated. Striving for balance is a profound and pervasive aspect of the human condition. Balance is an ancient concern and a cornerstone belief in eastern religion. In Buddhism, as illustrated by Siddartha's journey, it is called the *Middle Way*. In Confucianism balance is defined through the concept of *Yin-Yang*. Yin represents shade, darkness, cold, negativity and weakness. The Yang stands in opposition and reflects light, heat, positivity and strength. All change in the universe results from the interaction of these two forces. This passage from the *Tao Te Ching* expresses the movement created by the pressure of the opposites.

> All things bear the shade on their backs
> And the sun in their arms;
> By the blending of breath
> From the sun and the shade,
> Equilibrium comes to the world.

This same sense of movement through the reconciliation of opposites can be seen in Western thought as well. The most notable example is in the *dialectic* articulated by the German philosopher G. W. F. Hegel. Continuing and expanding upon philosophical systems that date to Plato and Aristotle, Hegel proposed that intellectual development is continually generated through a process of thesis, which gives rise to its opposite or antithesis. As a result of this conflict, a new balance emerges in the form of a synthesis. Thus movement is a product of the reconciliation or balancing of opposites.

The same movement can even be found in the statistics. It's a phenomenon called *regression to the mean*. The phenomenon occurs whenever researchers have a non-random sample from a population and two measures that are imperfectly correlated. In such situations, there is a tendency for individuals scoring especially high or low to regress toward the mean when they retake the same test.

The effect was seen dramatically in an Air Force study into the most effective teaching methods for instructor pilots. Despite mountains of research to the contrary, instructor pilots believed that trainees were more responsive to "butt chewings" than to positive reinforcement. Their argument was thus; when a student pilot completed a maneuver particularly well and was praised, his next effort almost invariably resulted in a lower level of performance. However, when chewed out for a poor maneuver, the student almost invariably improved on the next try.

The regression effect reveals that similar performance is to be expected in both situations even if the instructor says nothing at all. In fact, the tendency to regress toward the mean will occur in almost all situations. While researchers can correct for the regression effect, it provides an instructive model of how human behavior consistently pulls in from the extremes to find a comfortable "mean." The mean moves, but it moves slowly and only through many iterations.

Balance is also a biological fact. Called *homeostasis*, it is the tendency of a biological system to maintain a state of equilibrium. Homeostasis applies to an organism's internal balance and can be seen in the body's self-regulation of temperature, cell growth, body fluid composition, and hormone and acid levels. Cravings are understood as the body's attempts to correct an imbalance. The concept is also operative on a larger scale. In nature, a balance is maintained between communities of organisms. This is commonly seen in the equilibrium between numbers of predators and prey found in the wild. The Gaia hypothesis is an even broader extension of homeostasis and reflects the planet's self-regulating tendencies.

The yearning for balance grips people at the most elemental levels. It is a biological, spiritual and intellectual drive that continually shapes behavior in obvious and subtle ways. It's seen in conflict resolution efforts and conflict avoidance strategies. It's behind the perpetual move for conformity and the resistance to new or extreme ways of thinking or behaving. That's why change comes slowly.

Extreme ideas will always be resisted and on those occasions where they hold sway, it will be temporary. The moderating forces will move inexorably to the middle ground. Change will come because balance is dynamic. It is a motivating force, but one which "makes haste slowly." Colloquial references to the "swinging pendulum" attest to this. People anticipate a restoration of equilibrium, but rarely do they expect to be restored to the same place. The pendulum swings slightly forward with each move toward the center point.

One final point bears consideration: The relentless, progressive drive for balance always creates something new. This is the increasing mean, or Hegel's synthesis. Here it is rather inelegantly called the *"third thing."* The third thing occurs effortlessly in all human interactions. At its best, it is seen when groups build upon a single idea. In the synergy created, each new variation of the original idea becomes something different, better, larger than the first thought. At its worst it is seen in arguments that seem to "take on a life of their own." Whether positive or negative, the third thing is always developing and must be respected for the power it yields.

The second principle is to, "*stay balanced.*" The most successful leaders will stay alert for the middle way. They will productively glean from the extremes and create a robust center.

The Third Principle: Simplicity

William was born in Ockham, a city southwest of London, just off what is now junction 10 of the M25 with the A3. Of course, at the time of his birth in 1285, there was no M25 or A3. In fact the city itself may have been called "Occam," as both spellings appear in the records. Despite being a small town imprecisely spelled, Ockham's favorite son became one of the 14th century's most influential theologians, philosophers and political commentators. His legacy, far from being medieval, is remarkably fresh, and by today's standards, even liberal.

Not much is known of his earliest years though it is believed he was sixteen when he entered the Franciscan Order. His initial convent education, which focused heavily on logic, shaped his entire career. Later he would study theology at Oxford and lecture there between 1317 and 1319. His strong opinions, however, drew him into conflict with the faculty and he left before obtaining his master's degree.

In an age highly suspicious of divergent opinions, it was not surprising that by 1324 he was summoned to Avignon by the Pope. Not easily intimidated, William mounted a spirited defense of his positions and in the process became even more convinced of their accuracy. A practical, as well as scholarly man, he fled Avignon in 1328 and settled in Munich under the protection of Ludwig of Bavaria. He continued his controversial writing and lecturing until his death from the Black plague in 1349.

Among his more interesting positions are the beliefs that Christians have the right to express opposition to the Church and that the Pope is fallible. He went further and suggested that a pope, king, emperor or *any* leader could be deposed for violating the rights of those they lead. Still further, he maintained that secular governments do not require Church approval; that the civic and property rights of non-Christians should be respected; and that women, as well as men, should participate in Church governance.

But William's most enduring legacy is what has come to be called, "Ockham's Razor." The razor states, "Pluralitas non est ponenda sine necessitas." *That is, plurality shouldn't be posited, or, assumed without necessity.* In a related saying (sometimes called the razor as well), Ockham noted, "Frustra fit per plura, quod potest fieri per pauciora," or, *"it is vain to do with more what can be done with less."* These twin concepts are linked to a third Ockham theorem; that is, *explanations of the unknown should first be sought in the known.* Together, they form the basis for the third *Fifth Station* principle.

The third principle is *simplicity*. A shorthand version of the razor might be, *"keep it simple."* When complexity is added to a relationship, process or organization without good reason, the result is usually a loss of focus or clarity. Roles become blurred, goals are uncertain and success is haphazard. In the Eighties, a popular corporate strategy was the acquisition of businesses unrelated or tangential to the company's core business. The result was usually disastrous. The central executive staff often had difficulty managing diverse businesses with which they were unfamiliar. Efforts to consolidate core support functions frequently proved overwhelming and distracted by the effort, the core business suffered. The problem was simply that the parent company had become unnecessarily complex.

Bureaucracies are prime violators of the principle. Clinging to management structures designed in the 19th century to help the railways run on time, many organizations maintain complex supervisory relations that unnecessarily slow work. Even in companies that have slashed middle management, the supervisory web remains—although often working under a new name. Team captains may have replaced department heads, but someone is still signing leave requests.

The reengineering movement brought a significant corrective to this kind of workplace complexity. While the quality initiative asked, "how can we do it better," reengineering asked, "should you do it at all?" The question is an excellent filter for leaders striving for simplicity. It should be asked before any decision is made or action taken. It is a modern extension of the Razor that helps "keep it simple."

The Razor's twin concept is equally important in maintaining simplicity. It argues that when all else is equal, the simpler of two alternatives is always to be preferred. This concept has deep roots in western thought. In *Physics*, Aristotle states, "for the more limited, if adequate, is always preferable," and later, "for if the consequences are the same, it is always better to assume the more limited antecedent." We know this intuitively.

The clear, concise and understandable will always produce better results. A specific goal increases the chances of achieving the specified result. A process that generates a product in five steps will always be more effective than one that produces a product of equal quality in ten steps. Machines with fewer parts are more reliable than machines with many parts. And so it goes.

Meeting guides, time management planners, and decision-making models are routinely embraced and discarded because they promise big gains, but turn out to be too complicated. Perhaps the best visual reminder of our preference for the simple alternative can be found in almost any park. Despite paved and elaborately landscaped walkways, hard pack footpaths usually mark the most direct route. If the answer to our first question, "should we do it," is, "yes," the second question is, "what's the most direct route?" And to preserve simplicity, when we find it, we'll take it.

Ockham's third point essentially says that the search for the unknown must begin with the known. While the point seems obvious, it is often overlooked. Sir Arthur Conan Doyle acknowledged as much when he noted, "It is a capital mistake to theorize before one has data. Insensibly, one begins to twist facts to suit theories, instead of theories to suit facts."

When we begin with the bedrock of what we know, we can save phenomenal amounts of time that would otherwise be wasted in trial, speculation and error.

Unnecessary complexity is added in the search for additional resources. But data regarding the known should not be confused with specific detail. If, for example, WYSINWYG is part of your frame of reference, that is, something you *know*, it becomes a valuable tool in shaping alternatives. It will save effort by encouraging you to anticipate and plan for the unexpected while looking for new assets hidden in your current resources. Since you *know* the principle of WYSINWYG, it will help you explore the unknown. By actively using what we *know* to be true about people, teams and organizations we can virtually guarantee success at minimal cost.

The third principle, then, is, *"keep it simple."* Simplicity requires only three things from leaders. First, begin with what you *know*. Accumulate data, both objective and subjective, in order to determine your goal. Secondly, find and follow the most direct path to the goal. Select the process with the fewest elements that will produce a quality product. Third, before you do anything, be sure it is something you want to do. Simplicity pays off in focus, clarity, accuracy and time spent doing only the essential. Though William of Ockham has provided the basis for this discussion, the final word will go to an American:

> Simplicity, simplicity, simplicity! I say, let your affairs be as two or three, and not a hundred or a thousand; instead of a million count half a dozen, and keep your accounts on your thumbnail.

> Henry David Thoreau
> *Walden*, 'Where I lived and What I Lived For"

CHAOS

Blame it on the apple. Legend has it that Isaac Newton was innocently seated beneath an apple tree when a falling piece of fruit startled him into some of the most amazing scientific insights ever recorded in the western world. An English mathematician and scientist, Newton invented calculus and formulated theories of universal gravitation, terrestrial mechanics and color. In his monumental 1687 work, *Principia Mathematica*, he applies his theories to the movement of planets, the motion of comets and the action of tides.

The accuracy of Newton's formulas led scientists to adopt a view of the universe as a deterministic and well-ordered place. The assumption was that if you knew the natural *laws* and a system's *present condition*, you could accurately *predict* the system's future behavior. Accepted was the belief that because measurement could never be completely accurate, small variations or approximations in the calculations would not significantly alter the final results. For example, an investment of $100 in a certificate of deposit compounded at 6% annually will yield $179.08 after ten years. The same money compounded at 6.25% annually will return $183.35. Thus, small changes in the initial conditions produce relatively small changes in the final condition.

This view spurred much of the initial interest in computers. After all, in a deterministic universe, our ability to make ever more accurate predictions is limited only by our ability to compute ever more complex equations. Thus, while weather forecasters can predict that a Houston summer will be hotter than a Houston winter, they can't tell you on the 4th of January if it will rain on the 4th of July. The *periodic* nature of the seasons makes the broad prediction possible, but the complexity of daily factors makes determining specific weather patterns a challenge. Computers hold the promise of mastering such complexity and in the process provide us, among other things, with vital information about when to plan the company picnic.

Blame it on the shortcut. Edward Lorenz was a research meteorologist at the Massachusetts Institute of Technology. In 1960, using a primitive Royal McBee computer, he digitized the weather in a search for a Newtonian deterministic forecasting model. Tinkering with weather variables, he produced orderly, wave-like patterns that cycled, though never repeated identically. One afternoon, wishing to reexamine a particular sequence, he took a shortcut. Rather than starting the sequence over again, he began it in the middle, using numbers from the earlier printout to provide the *initial condition*. An hour later he checked the computer's progress and was surprised to find that the new pattern diverged sharply from the first. He later discovered that this decidedly *un*-Newtonian behavior was a direct result of a *very* Newtonian assumption.

For convenience, the printouts used by Lorenz printed numbers to only three decimal places, while the computer actually stored numbers to six decimal places. Thus, Lorenz entered an initial condition of .506, while the actual condition at that point in the sequence was .506127. The computer performed in a purely deterministic fashion. As was to be expected, slight differences in the initial condition launched the calculations in slightly different directions. The surprise was the chaotic divergence of patterns. Lorenz had revealed that systems that never reached stability, or that never quite repeated themselves, were inherently unpredictable. From this was born the *Butterfly Effect*.

The *Butterfly Effect* suggests that a butterfly flapping its wings in Tiananmen Square today may produce a thunderstorm in Central Park next month. This is because something as slight as the flapping of a butterfly's wings will produce atmospheric variations that in turn, influence the atmosphere in other ways that create a cumulative and ultimately random effect. Even though the initial conditions, the atmosphere with and without the flapping, are nearly identical, they can create vastly different outcomes. This phenomenon became one of the first tenets of *chaos theory* and is called *sensitive dependence on initial conditions*. It stands as a counterpoint to Newtonian determinism and means that small changes in the initial condition of a nonperiodic, or non-repeating system, can dramatically alter the system's long-term behavior. These dramatic alterations make the system chaotic or unpredictable.

To get a better sense of nonperiodic systems, let's return to our CD investment. The investment was *deterministic*. Given knowledge of the initial conditions ($100 invested, 6% annual return over ten years) the outcome was entirely predictable—$179.08 saved. But determinism fails if the prediction is about the *buying power* of the investment in ten years.

Assuming an annual inflation rate of 2%, the investment is worth $146.91. If inflation rises to 7%, the buying power is about $91.04. Of course, there could be deflation during the period. New technologies might drive commodity prices down or natural disaster could drive food prices up. There are an endless number of variations that could influence the buying power of the $100 investment.

The complexity derives from the fact that we must now calculate not only annual *return*, but also annual *value*. Because value is dependent upon so many variables, it will never be a stable rate, as is annual return. Nor is it *periodic*, with the same variables identically repeating themselves in the economy each year for ten years. A host of differing conditions can drive value in madly chaotic directions.

Lorenz recognized that chaotic systems existed everywhere. Weather, epidemiology, ecology are just a few of the natural systems sensitively dependent upon initial conditions. In fact, orderly systems appear to be in a distinct minority. Chaos is the standard for systems. But he saw beyond the randomness. He developed simpler models using only three instead of the original twelve equations in his weather model that still produced random behavior. When he graphed the behavior, instead of getting a Jackson

Pollack style splatter, he found a unique pattern. The output of the system always remained on a double spiral. Because the system was nonperiodic, and thus never exactly repeated itself, the trajectory never intersected itself.

Previously only two types of order were known. Systems were either stable, with no changes in the variables, or periodic, in which systems endlessly looped. The Lorenz model was something altogether new. He called it the Lorenz attractor, which stated that beneath even apparently random behavior lurked order of some kind.

Newton, chaos and Lorenz Attractors may seem a bit far removed from leadership and team dynamics until we take a closer look. Newton described a deterministic, well-ordered system. If you knew the rules and could approximate the initial condition, you could approximate the system's future behavior. Of course, the simpler the system, the easier this is to do. If the variables always remain unchanged or the system periodically repeats itself, predictions can be made with great accuracy. After all, without the benefit of computers or the Hubble telescope, astronomers in 1910 were able to correctly predict the arrival of Halley's comet in 1986.

Lorenz, on the other hand, found a way to describe complex, constantly changing systems that appear entirely random. We know that chaotic systems are very sensitive to initial conditions. Slight changes in the initial condition can produce vastly different results, making the systems unpredictable. However, he discovered that these apparently chaotic systems are actually bound in a type of order. This order was first graphed as a double spiral—the Lorenz attractor. Thus, chaotic systems are actually deterministic. To create the attractor, something must be determining the system's behavior. The net result is that *there is order in chaos*, though it is not easy to apprehend, and actually appears to be random.

Most organizations today are functionally Newtonian and consequently very confused by the chaos they experience. Armed with "one size fits all," human resources and relations assumptions, they attempt to shape employee behavior toward predictable ends, and expect predictable results.

They are amazed when cross-the-board increases don't improve morale beyond the afternoon of the morning they are given. They puzzle over why the April employee of the month is being counseled for a bad attitude in June. They don't appreciate why it takes employees six months to recover from downsizing or layoff announcements made any time between November first and December 31st. They can't understand why the off-site meeting that energized everyone for a year last time, is a bust this year. Most of all, they just don't see why so much time is eaten up by personnel problems that wouldn't *be* problems if people just did what they were supposed to do!

The answer, of course, is that any human system is a chaotic system. The Newtonian formula—know the rules, know the present condition, get the predictable (desired) results—just doesn't apply. If it did, giving a merit raise would go something like this: (1) Rule: money motivates and thus will increase productivity; (2) Mr. And Ms. Werquer haven't had a raise in six years and deserve one; (3) raises awarded and happy employees cheerfully do more work. That rarely happens.

We *do* know that the motivational value of the raise decreases algorithmically from the moment it's awarded. We also know that some other things can happen. Mr. and Ms. Werquer might compare raises and while one feels cheated, the other feels the raise is too little too late and resents it. Team members who don't get raises may be upset and as a result, group productivity declines. Mr. Werquer might blow the raise on a car he can't afford and be distracted for the next five years by financial problems. Ms. Werquer might appreciate the raise, but as it's deserved, doesn't feel she owes the company anything more. Just possibly, the raises are appreciated and everyone is happy—*for now*. This is the bad news. The good news is that there is order in the human chaos.

It is important to remember that Newtonian expectations produce WYSIWYG thinking. If applications of rules under well-known conditions produce predictable results, then what you see *is* what you get. But human systems are chaotic and the principle of WYSINWYG reigns. What you see is *never* what you get. There are so many variables involved when dealing with individuals, that savvy leaders will remember that there is always more going on than they can ever hope to apprehend. They will remember that, in the spirit of WYSINWYG, everyone is sensitively dependent on initial conditions and that there are no "one size fits all," solutions. Even approaches that worked with someone before may not produce the same result because people are naturally dynamic and the process of growth and maturation will alter expectations.

On with the good news. Though human systems are chaotic, every individual displays identifiable *paradigms* of behavior. A paradigm is a pattern or model. It is a way of thinking about or doing things.

Newton's publication of the *Principia* created a new scientific paradigm. It gave others a system of examples about the natural order that fostered theories, laws, measurements and applications. It gave scientists a starting point when thinking about subjects such as Newtonian Dynamics.

On a much more personal scale, everyone displays paradigms, tiny rituals, in their day-to-day behavior. People brush their teeth, put on their clothes, go to work, interact and do dozens of others things every day in the identical way. We do these common things unconsciously; it's just a part of daily routine.

While we aren't always aware of our own paradigmatic behavior, those around us usually *are*. Co-workers can spot your sour mood while you're still in the parking lot. Your spouse can tell you have good news by the way you walk in the door. You can tell when it's a bad report card day before even saying hello to your child. Raising these paradigms to consciousness is a prerequisite for dealing with them.

A gentleman who chronically locked his keys in the car was asked to study his *car-parking* paradigm. He observed that whenever he parked his car, he immediately switched off the engine; pulled the key halfway out of the ignition and in the same move opened the door. With the door opened, he gathered his briefcase, coat or whatever else he had with him, removed the key from the ignition and left the car. It was only when he raised this behavior to consciousness that he realized that pulling the key halfway out of the ignition was to keep the door buzzer from sounding while he gathered his materials.

The paradigm worked fine unless he was in a particular hurry, or took an extra long time gathering his materials, or was just generally distracted. Then, in the absence of the sounding buzzer, he would forget to remove the key before exiting and locking himself out. Armed with the knowledge of the paradigm, he was able to change it for the better.

Paradigms are at work on a social scale as well. Forty years ago most Americans smoked and the only known "no smoking" areas were adjacent to highly combustible materials. Smoking was glamorous; smoking made you appear more confident, smoking was definitely "in." Today you can recognize smokers as those pathetic individuals huddled twenty-five feet from the entrance to the building furtively puffing away in the hopes of not being recognized. Our paradigms about smoking changed only when raised to consciousness through public debate and when non-smoking became a desirable alternative.

This is a key point about paradigm change. A paradigm—personal, social or organizational—will not change unless another paradigm has been found to take its place. While people will tinker and experiment with another approach, they won't change their paradigm unless they become dissatisfied and convinced that an alternative is better. Smoking provides another good example. Given the vast numbers of people, who have successfully quit smoking, it's not an impossible habit to break. But people who quit forever are those who decided to switch to a non-smoking paradigm. In other words, they *wanted* to quit. Those who quit, but aren't convinced it's a better alternative are very likely to start smoking again. This will be the case with any paradigm. In order to change it, you must be *absolutely convinced* that the new paradigm is superior to the old.

Leaders will immediately recognize the significance of paradigms. For one thing, you'll recognize that you signal your intentions all the time. In order to send the right signals, you have to be aware of what you're doing. A department head in a small manufacturing firm, spread terror among his staff by acting distant and unusually serious at a time when layoffs were rumored. He was actually obsessing about a new home purchase that would severely stretch his budget, but in the absence of that information, the staff assumed the worse. Effective leaders will remember that their unconscious behavior, sometimes called, "style," will often provide the sensitive dependence on initial conditions described in chaos theory and produce totally unexpected results among their teams.

Leaders will also recognize that paradigmatic behavior in others can be identified and managed. Once you start thinking about your own behavioral rituals, it becomes easy to observe rituals in others. *Observe* is the key word here because it has already been noted that we easily pick up on the paradigms of others. When this is the case, we most often react to the signals broadcast (usually unwittingly) by the other person.

An observer is sensitive to ritual behavior and anticipates it. This anticipation again reflects the WYSINWYG principle. Most people watching someone in the office bearing down on them, broadcasting "bad mood," will go into a desperate defensive mode. This response is akin to an organizational, "Dive! Dive! Dive!" But the careful observer withholds judgment.

It *could* be a bad mood brought on by a pet stained carpet at home. Chaos theory teaches us that a premature hostile response might produce an extraordinarily disproportionate reaction. Everyday thousands of people become antagonistic with others over things that have nothing to do with either of them. They are simply reacting to paradigms rather than anticipating and managing their responses.

These behavioral paradigms are relatively easy to spot and easy to deal with. After all, everyone is able to tolerate a few quirks in themselves and others. But there is something deeper and far more profound going on as well. We frequently use paradigms without the awareness that they reflect our worldview, believing that our view is the *only* view. This does not reflect arrogance; instead it's our acceptance of the status quo without the understanding that everyone defines the status quo in terms of his or her own peculiar perspective.

It is one thing to realize that you always put the creamer in your cup before adding coffee, and quite another to recognize that you routinely make decisions based on subjective rather than objective data. It's knowledge of this deeper structure that will unlock the power of your organization and impose order on the apparently chaotic behavior of the group.

The Secret Order

The belief that there is *chaos* in human knowledge has been with us for a long time. Our old friend Ockham, ruminating in the 14th century speculated that all knowledge was the product of a two-part process. The first part he called *simple knowledge*. Simple knowledge was acquired directly through our five senses or abstractly through our sixth sense or what we might call intuition. *Complex knowledge* followed as the result of the judgments we applied to our simple knowledge. This was knowledge in the strictest sense as it gave meaning to our experience. As we shall shortly see, Ockham's orderly philosophical considerations would find practical application in the 20th century.

It began with Carl Gustav Jung. Jung, a Swiss psychiatrist, was a contemporary of Freud and founder of the analytical psychology school. He broke with Freud in 1912, with the publication of this landmark work, *Psychology of the Unconscious*. In this book, Jung theorized two dimensions of the unconscious. The first is the *personal*, which includes all the forgotten or repressed aspects of one's mental or material life. The second dimension is the *collective* unconscious. It includes the communal memory of all human experience. Though deeply buried in the psyche, the collective unconscious is reflected in images, symbols and stories found in our dreams, folklore, religion and mythology. Jung called these images, symbols and stories *archetypes*.

Essentially, archetypes are the *paradigms* by which we can explore the collective unconscious. Like the paradigms just discussed, Jung's archetypes reflect form rather than content. An archetype is a predisposition or *preference* for looking at something in a certain way. There are many archetypes, but some of the most easily recognized are the hero, the shadow, the wise man, the fool, the magician, the trickster, and the mother and the father.

Archetypes can also reflect processes such as the journey (series of steps toward the attainment of a goal) or rebirth (revelation, reincarnation or regeneration). Much of Jung's thinking entails what we have already identified as the second principle, *balance*. Personal development is a matter of reconciling opposites and discovering a common middle ground. The greatest individual challenge for anyone then is to find harmony between the conscious and unconscious. Of course, for Jung, recognition of the archetype provided a kind of order in which such harmony became possible. In discussing archetypes Jung noted, "In all chaos there is cosmos, *in all disorder a secret order.*"

Jung went a long way toward making the secret order in chaos accessible when, in 1921, he published, *Psychological Types*. In this work, Jung theorized, on the basis of extensive observation, that everyone uses four basic mental processes in daily living: sensing, intuition, thinking and feeling. In typical Jungian fashion, the four actually represent two sets of opposing pairs. The first pair, *sensing (S)* and *intuition (N)*, reflects how people *perceive* the world around them. The second pair, *thinking (T)* and *feeling (F)* reflect how people make *decisions* about the data that they perceive.

While everyone uses all four, Jung believed individuals have innate preferences for different processes. Preferences are innate and are exercised without thinking. A good example is "handedness." Take a moment and write your signature on a piece of paper. Now write it using your other hand. One way is easy, effortless and natural. The other way is difficult, forced and awkward. Right or left-handedness is an innate preference. In the same way, the structure of people's personalities reflects innate preferences. Thus, at the very core of human personality, Jung is suggesting four possible combinations of how people prefer to gather data and make decisions: *sensing/thinking (ST), sensing/feeling (SF), intuition/thinking (NT), and intuition/feeling (NF).*

In addition to the four processes, Jung also believed that people orient themselves toward life with either an *extraverted (E)* or *introverted (I) attitude.* Like the mental processes, orientation is innate, and individuals demonstrate a clear preference for one attitude over the other. The addition of this scale expands our possible personality types to eight: *EST, IST, ESF, ISF, ENT, INT, ENF, and INF.*

Jung's theory of psychological type found zealous disciples in the persons of Katherine Briggs and Isabel Meyers. This mother and daughter team had been keen students of psychological type for 16 years when the outbreak of World War II suggested a unique application of the theory. Briggs and Meyers believed that type would be an ideal tool for determining the vocational placement of women newly arrived to the work place. After all, if women accepted positions well suited to their personalities, they would be more likely to do a good job and to stay in the job than if they were dissatisfied.

The women discovered that no such instrument existed, and so began to develop one. By 1943 they had completed the first series of questions that would become the Meyers Briggs Type Indicator, or perhaps more familiarly, the MBTI. (The Meyers-Briggs Type Indicator and MBTI are registered trademarks of Consulting Psychologist Press, Inc.) After over a decade of research and experimentation, the MBTI was published as a research instrument in 1956. Since that time, the instrument has been continually refined and accepted worldwide as a highly reliable and valid tool.

During the course of their research, Briggs and Meyers extended Jung's model of personality by making explicit a fourth scale that had only been implied in Jung's theory. That scale describes *orientation to the outer world* and deals with preferences for *judgment (J)* or *perception (P)*. The fourth scale created the possibility of exploring personality as one of *sixteen* unique types produced by the eight preferences. The sixteen types and their relationship are displayed in the Type table below.

ISTJ	ISFJ	INFJ	INTJ
ISTP	ISFP	INFP	INTP
ESTP	ESFP	ENFP	ENTP
ESTJ	ESFJ	ENFJ	ENTJ

Before examining the four scales, a few points about personality type should be underscored. First, type is a way of describing *normal* behavior. The sixteen possible types reflect sixteen equally legitimate ways of gathering data and acting on that data. Secondly, type is a *paradigm* for bringing order to human behavior that otherwise seems chaotic or random. The MBTI is a means of describing that order and equipping everyone with a common vocabulary for discussing behavior. Thirdly, type helps us appreciate that our way is not the only way.

Jung said, "If one does not understand a person, one tends to regard him as a fool." Type is a powerful tool for identifying and leveraging commonalties and differences. Finally, type satisfies our three principles. It certainly operates with the *WYSINWYG* principle. Random behavior is actually *very* ordered. Recognizing type dynamics will help individuals and teams respect differences and be open to new ways of looking at old problems. Type also involves *balance*. Healthy personal development includes gaining facility with your non-preferred functions and attitudes. Good decision-making will call for striking a balance between the opposing pairs. Type is also *simple*. With only four scales, the theory is easily taught and applied. It provides a speedy and intuitively acceptable decision-making filter. Finally, it provides a common sense framework in which to examine and impact interpersonal relations.

Our discussion to this point has been aimed at demonstrating the underlying order of apparently chaotic human behavior. The descriptions of the type scales and the key word comparisons that follow provide only the briefest of introductions to the wealth of insight available to individuals and teams that take time to access and apply the information.

The Data-gathering Scale: Sensing and Intuition

Data-gathering and *decision-making* are the two most important aspects of the personality paradigm. These two *processes* are at the core of everything we do as human beings. There is not an aspect of life that is not shaped by the way we gather data and then make decisions about it. The functions work sequentially and data-gathering is, of course, the first. The preferences for data-gathering are either *sensing* or *intuition*.

Sensing simply means gathering information through human senses such as sight, sound, taste touch and smell. Someone with this preference finds such experience-based data the most reliable source for making decisions. Naturally, people with a preference for sensing pay close attention to their environment.

They focus on reality. They are oriented to the present and rely on the *here and now* for accurate information. They notice detail and put much stock in the specifics of an event or idea. They value experience because it leads to applied knowledge. They like to see the practical applications of theory before accepting it as worthwhile.

People who prefer sensing are able to easily spot linear sequences and generally prefer to receive information this way. They are often called *concrete* thinkers. They like to, "make *sense* of things." The benefits of accurately knowing one's environment are obvious, but this type also faces some problems. Suspicion of the untried is one of the greatest weaknesses of this preference. With a strong focus on data that is practical, proven and factual, sometimes innovations or "wild" but potentially valuable ideas can be discounted. Since sensors reflect roughly 70% of the population, there is an inherent bias for sense-oriented data as the foundation for decision-making. Also, there is a possible bias against intuitive data gatherers who might be perceived as having their "heads in the clouds" rather than their "feet on the ground." Such a bias can close the door to any opportunity that doesn't fit the current way of thinking.

Intuitive data gatherers are very much in tune with finding ways that don't fit the current way of thinking. They tend to look for and find the "big picture." They are future oriented and relish the world of possibilities. They easily draw connections between objects and recognize underlying relationships not readily apparent to others. They notice and particularly enjoy discovering the theory behind an application.

This ability to see abstract relationships makes intuitives natural innovators. They seek new opportunities everywhere and imaginatively apply prior experiences in unique ways. Rather than linear thinkers, intuitives tend to be web-like thinkers. There is often a random and impulsive quality in their data search. They spring from topic to topic driven by an excitement for finding unusual relations. Rather than asking, "Why," intuitives tend to ask, "Why not?"

Representing only 30% of the adult population, intuitives are very much in the minority. Beyond simply being dismissed by sensors as "dreamers," intuitives run some significant risks. The broad scope of the intuitive can lead to disaster if facts are not accounted for in the data used for decision-making. In their zeal for the new and different, intuitives can lose sight of what is actually possible given current resources. Intuitives can also lose interest in things that are too "concrete." The resultant lack of attention to detail can prove disastrous when a decision is finally implemented.

The best data-gathering will take into account both points of view. Decisions must be practical to the extent that they can be reasonably implemented. However, there must also be vision or stretch. It is the stretch that moves individuals and organizations forward to new opportunity and potential.

Data-gathering

Sensing	Intuition
Use the Five Senses	Use the Sixth Sense-Hunches
Real	Possible
Factual	Theoretical
Practical	Conceptual
Utilitarian	Insightful
Detail	Abstract
Sequential	Random
Present-Oriented	Future-Oriented

The Decision-making Scale: Thinking and Feeling

Once data has been gathered, decisions *will* be made. Sometimes the decisions are significant, while at other times they are routine and slip by unnoticed. The important thing to remember is that something is always done with the collected data. How people arrive at their decisions is the business of the decision-making scale. The two preferences for decision-making are *thinking* and *feeling*. Jung's choice of language is somewhat unfortunate. The implication of the word "feeling" is that it is an emotional or affective function. That's not the case. Both thinking and feeling are *rational* processes for reaching effective decisions.

Objectivity is the core of decision-making for those who prefer the *thinking* function. They typically adopt an impersonal stance and evaluate all data logically and rationally. They strive to be reasonable and consequently exercise a high standard of fairness. They are expert problem solvers because they systematically apply cause and effect analysis or other logical tools to resolve difficulties. When they reach a decision it's almost always crystal clear to others. Though you may not agree with the decision, you will have no difficulty understanding how the decision was reached.

The thinking function works equally well with data gathered both through sensing and intuition. It is easy to see how fact oriented sense data lends itself to logical, objective analysis. For many people truth and fact are virtually synonymous. Yet when the thinking preference is applied to intuitively gathered data, it gains credibility with sensors. When objective standards are used to evaluate abstract concepts, the concepts become available to a larger audience.

Approximately 50% of the population are *thinking deciders*. Interestingly, two thirds of the thinkers are male. Two significant problems derive from this preference. The first, obviously, is that decisions made with this preference may contain a gender bias—effectively screening out the preferences of women in terms of decision-making. The second problem is that in the pursuit of objective fairness, important subjective considerations may be ignored. Because of this, thinkers might be unfairly perceived as cold or heartless—*Mr. Spocks* if you will.

Feeling is the opposite form of decision-making. Again, feeling does not refer to an emotional style of decision-making. Rather, it's a preference that places subjective values at the core of the process. People who share this preference tend to equate truth, not with fact, but with *values. Feeling deciders* are people-focused and believe that the best decisions are those that fully account for human needs. They are adept at looking beyond the facts of a situation and determining the human impact of a decision.

Feelers see shades of gray where thinkers might find the simple black and white of cause and effect. For them, a decision that disrupts the harmony of the work place will never be a good decision. A decision that ignores a human cost is never acceptable. While feelers strive for harmony rather than clarity, their decisions, when examined, reflect an internal logic. Though a decision may run counter to the assembled "facts," it will be rationally consistent with the feelers personal principles.

Fifty percent of the population are feelers and of that number, two thirds are female. As with thinkers, this representation can lead to gender bias. It is also problematic when thinkers dismiss the logic employed by feelers as "soft" or "warm and fuzzy." Such dismissive responses, however, overlook the fact that many programs are undermined by silent disagreement. Silent disagreement or passive aggressiveness are common responses when decisions are implemented that alienate those effected. The "logic" applied by feeling deciders, though baffling to many thinking deciders is essential for effective relationships, teams and organizations.

As with the other preferences, the best results will always be produced when both ends of the scale are fully considered. Every decision should pass the test for logic, objectivity and reasonableness as well as the test for consistency with values, human cost and the promotion of harmony.

Decision-making

Thinking	Feeling
Objective	Subjective
Clarify	Harmonize
Logical Analysis	Value Analysis
Cause and Effect	Impact on People
Reasonable	Empathetic
Analytical	Sympathetic
Just	Humane
Critique	Appreciate

The Energizing Scale: Extraversion and Introversion

Energizing is a *behavioral* scale. It deals with the way people process information. Preferences here determine *where* and *how* the other preferences are acted out. The *where* is either social, on a public stage or reflective, in one's private thoughts. The *how* is either verbal or thoughtful, perhaps through the written word. Each approach is distinctively different in the way experience is processed.

Extraverts account for approximately 70% of the population. This means that they tend to focus on things outside themselves as a means of processing information. They are generally expressive and are inspired by social interactions. Extraverts are great talkers. In fact, *talking through* a problem is a favorite system for drawing conclusions. In meetings, extraverts will excitedly move through a topic, frequently "piggy-backing" off the ideas of someone else as they synergistically explore a subject. The mere action of saying something is in and of itself helpful. They learn best by actually doing a thing and talking about it.

Extraverts are naturally initiative in activities and in personal relationships. Because energy is drawn from interacting with others, they tend to have many relationships and often develop a broad range of interests. Extraverts sometimes find themselves in trouble because of their volubility. Since talking things out is an active process, not everything that is said is meant as the final word on the subject. An extravert may give the impression of pronouncing a conclusion when in fact they are simply playing with a possibility. Not surprisingly, this can seem pretty overwhelming to an introvert.

Introverts look inward to process information. They rely on a personal world of thought and reflection. If extraverts talk things through, introverts *think them through*. Their approach is generally quiet. They *mull* ideas, play with them, measure them against their inner sense of experience. Though a reflective process, it is none-the-less an active one. The introvert may well conduct an inner dialog with the same ferocity that the most ardent extravert brings to a particularly juicy debate. The only difference is that one operates internally while the other operates externally.

As may be expected, the internal focus of the introvert often results in fewer, though at times closer, relationships. It also produces deeper understandings of subjects of interest. Representing only 30% of the population can cause problems for the introvert. Often their quiet approach is taken as a lack of interest or indifference by extraverts.

Real problems also develop when extraverts assume that silence on the part of an introvert signals assent. Late in a discussion an introvert often brings a sharp focus to a subject that was missed in all the activity of the extraverts. Not surprisingly, the introvert's silence followed by insight is often baffling to the extravert.

The extravert and introvert preferences reflect two vital aspects of team success. Teams must identify and discuss all pertinent data. They must also apply a brake to decision-making and fully reflect on the implications and consequences of their choices.

Energizing

Extraversion	Introversion
Talk It Through	Think It Over
Breadth	Depth
Act	Reflect
People and Things	Thoughts and Ideas
Get Moving	Settle Down
Outward	Inward
Interact	Concentrate
Many, Casual Friends	Fewer, Closer friends

Orientation to the Environment: Judging and Perceiving

This final scale is perhaps the most important in terms of the relationships between people. The preference for either *judging* or *perceiving* indicates the way in which you approach the world. It is your *operating style*. The preferences relate to either data-gathering or decision-making. If you are a judger, it means that you live your life in a *decision-making mode*. Perceivers on the other hand, operate in a *data-gathering mode*. Both are normal, but produce very different results.

Reaching the decision point or *closure* is the goal of the judger. People exercising this preference tend to lead very orderly, planned lives. They like to "get on with things." They consider options, evaluate courses of action and then do it. This extends to the world of ideas as well. Judgers are likely to form an opinion and stick to it. In their methodical, systematic approach, they usually have no trouble finding the "right" and "wrong" of every situation. They tend not to like surprises, preferring instead to control and monitor their environment. They plan work in advance to avoid last minute crises. Judgers respect schedules and appreciate deadlines. They are comfortable with structure. About 55% of the population are judgers.

Perceivers, on the other hand, use the information gathering function as their operating style. They are, in effect, life-long seekers. Rather than controlling their environment, they actively explore it in a search for understanding. This approach tends to make them more spontaneous. They remain flexible on most issues and easily adapt to changing requirements as new data becomes available. Instead of moving toward closure, perceivers prefer to have things remain open-ended. They remain tentative in order to be available for new options. For many perceivers, schedules, deadlines and especially plans are anathema. Unlike judgers who actively work to avoid crisis, perceivers tend to work best under "last minute" pressure. Many perceivers resist structure as too confining. Approximately 45% of the population are perceivers.

Because the numbers of judgers and perceivers are so close, the potential for interpersonal conflict is tremendous. They are in routine contact with each other and have the potential to drive one and other to absolute distraction. Judgers can't understand why perceivers wait until the last minute to complete an assignment that had ample lead-time. Perceivers are confused when judgers won't amend a plan based on pertinent new information.

Of course, as with the other preferences, a balance between the two is necessary for optimal performance. The judger's drive for closure can result in overlooking vital data that would warrant a different approach to the problem. Likewise, a perceiver who continually seeks new options may never produce a result. Teams must recognize the value of both approaches and self-consciously work to accommodate the other preference. Flexible or concurrent planning is a tool discussed later that provides a structure helpful in achieving this end.

Orientation to the Environment

Judging	Perceiving
Decision-making	Data-gathering
Planned	Spontaneous
Fixed	Flexible
Closure	Open-ended
Decisive	Tentative
Resolve	Seek
Ordered	Casual
Structured	Adaptive

Some Thoughts

As promised, this has been a quick overview of psychological type as developed by Jung, Briggs and Meyers. Its purpose here is to demonstrate the underlying order that can be found in human behavior. What once had seemed chaotic can now be seen as structured. Differences of opinion that had once seemed arbitrary can now be valued as important dimensions of data-gathering and decision-making. Though it has been said before, it's worth repeating; each type represents a normal, legitimate way of evaluating the same information. *Your* way is never more than one out of sixteen *possible* ways of looking at something. The fullest information and the best decisions will be made when the four scales are used in an appropriate *balance*. This order has two important implications for teams.

The first implication, with a nod to William of Ockham, I affectionately call *Ebert's Razor*. Ebert's Razor states that, "*people do what they want to do, and they want to do what works*." Without an appreciation for the order found in human behavior, this could sound cynical—but nothing could be farther from the truth.

The Razor recognizes that people have preferences for certain thought processes and behaviors of which they are not necessarily aware. From the surface paradigms of how people make coffee or wash their hair, to the deeper preferences for sensing over intuition, or feeling over thinking, everyone develops their personal routine for facing life. These routines become so comfortable that we don't invest very much psychic energy in their performance. For most situations we can operate on a type of psychological autopilot. This is an efficient way of living. We do what we want to do—*our* preferences, *our* paradigms—and we do them because they work.

The down side of the Razor is obvious. People often keep on doing what they want to do even when it *isn't* working. Remember that old paradigms are not likely to be replaced until dissatisfaction is created and a new paradigm found. This can lead to the *Titanic Effect*. By now almost everyone knows that the first lifeboats to leave the RMS Titanic were almost empty. People just couldn't believe the ship was sinking. *Common sense* dictated that you would be safer *on* a big boat than *in* a little one. Trans-Atlantic liners *didn't* sink and anyway, nothing *appeared* to be wrong. (They didn't know about WYSINWYG.) Of course, the ship *was* sinking and by the time everyone realized it, the first lifeboats were long gone and never to return.

Leaders will do well to remember that individuals and teams will behave in ways that have worked for them in the past. This will include behaviors that deal with success and behaviors that respond to crisis. It may lead otherwise sharp teams to ride the Titanic straight to the bottom. It may produce "irrational" responses to small issues. The best way to deal with the down side of this ordered human behavior and leverage upside is to raise the behavior to consciousness. Once people are aware of the their psychological preferences and behavioral paradigms, they can make better, *balanced* decisions on possible courses of action.

The second implication has to do with team structure. One of the most overlooked qualities of any team, company or culture is that it is composed of many human constituents. As soon as two or more people gather together, they seem to assume that there is a structure independent of their individual personalities. They assume there is a "team" standard that supercedes personality. They couldn't be more wrong.

A team is the embodiment of the Chaos tenet of sensitive dependence on initial conditions. The initial conditions are the psychological types of the individual members. Some not so simple math reveals that on a seven-member team, you can have almost 58,000,000 possible combinations of type. The various combinations can produce diametrically diverse solutions to the same data sets. They can result in teams that overlook the obvious or miss the implied; teams that solve the problem before understanding all the facts or teams that miss the deadline in a search for more data; teams that eloquently describe today and others that brilliantly illuminate tomorrow.

For this reason, leaders should work closely with members to understand the types represented. Teams should analyze their own composition and look for the inherent strengths and possible weaknesses. *Balance* is always to be desired but cannot be achieved without awareness.

The Secret Order of Teams

Up until now, our focus has been on the order underlying human behavior. We have seen that there is a structure beneath behavior that otherwise appears to be chaotic or random. It should come as no surprise, then, that organizations have an inherent order as well. Despite our best efforts at complexity, every organization engages in only three principle activities: *planning, developing and operating.* While almost every organization is highly skilled at masking these activities with endless divisions, sections, departments, and offices, the principle activities relentlessly continue just beneath the surface. Recognizing the activities and applying them appropriately can transform an organization's ability to perform. The transforming power comes from the fact that organizations do these three things whether or not they do them well.

Planning is frequently neglected and developing is often undernourished; yet the activities go on none-the-less. Effective organizations balance the three to produce optimal results, but most often they are done by default. Poor planning produces vague goals, which are implemented by people only "approximately" trained, and who can then produce only indifferent results.

This cyclic sense is important in understanding how the three work together because it is both simple and complex. A mandala is a good image for the relationship. A mandala is a geometric, repetitive design used as a meditative device by Hindus and Buddhists. The mandala's design is a means of inspiring revelation. Our organizational mandala begins with a circle. The circle tracks the movement from planning to developing to operating and back to planning. Thus we plan for outcomes, develop ourselves to fulfill the plan, exercise the plan, and then plan again based on our outcomes.

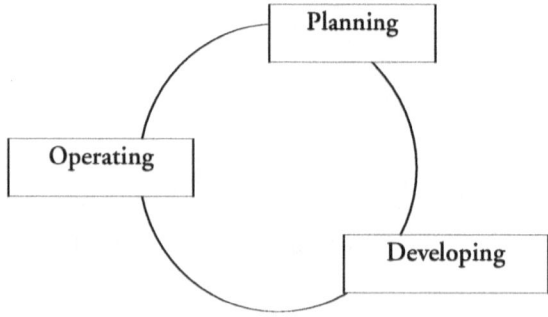

But there are circles within our circles. The act of planning requires a plan. It may involve developing new skills to design the plan. We then operate as we actually construct the plan and modify our next efforts on the basis of the first plan's design. Similarly, developing and operating contain circles within circles. Between the activities on our mandala, yonis are formed as the activities overlap with one another.

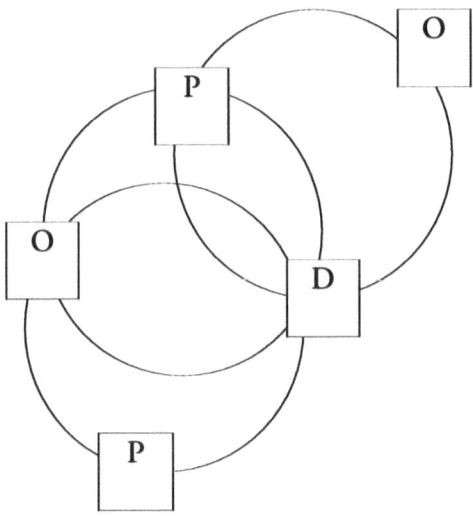

By this time you are either having an ecstatic experience or your head is spinning. In any case, our mandala image is simply a means of reflecting the complexity of the three interacting activities and their inherent order. Every team and organization is *always* engaged in one of the three activities

Planning is the first and probably the most neglected of the three. Within our culture there is a tendency to rush into *operating* long before an adequate plan can be developed. Said here for the first time, it will be repeated: *people don't spontaneously plan.* While we may routinely comment that someone or the team, "leaped into action," we never say that they "leaped into planning." When the stakes are high and time is short, we just want to get on with it!

"Getting on with it," though, is almost always a mistake. We know from exhaustive research and practical experience, that the best results follow a period of planning. Depending upon the task, the planning may be simple or elaborate. It may be reduced to a paradigm-like response or involve months of effort. The important point is that the goal is recognized and the approach determined. The most successful plans will consist of both pre-planning and concurrent planning. That is, the plan will anticipate what will happen and provide for a flexible, ongoing process that is responds to actual events. Overall planning processes that combine the features of *judging* and *perception* will produce a well-balanced, symmetrical approach to the goal.

Planning is a leadership function. It must occur before anything else happens, whether the CEO or shop floor quality improvement team is exercising the leadership involved. Though it can be delegated, the act of delegation should itself be a part of the leader's overall plan. Similarly, a team should never be assembled before initial planning takes place. Everything becomes more costly and complex in the absence of a plan. Despite the importance of planning, most leaders tend to shortchange the process. The boss, like everyone else, has more fun actually "doing it" than thinking or talking about it. This desire to be "hands on" is often behind micro-management. Very often the boss' intrusiveness has less to do with control than with a forlorn desire to still be involved with "it."

Despite our desire to be, "involved," no less an expert than Benjamin Franklin came down strongly in favor of planning. "I have always," he wrote in his *Autobiography*, "thought that one man of tolerable abilities may work great changes, and accomplish great affairs among mankind, if he first forms a good plan, and, cutting off all amusements or other employments that would divert his attention, make the execution of that same plan his sole study and business." The organization that recognizes *planning* as a principle activity and *balances* it with *developing* and *operating* will easily outstrip all competitors.

Developing is the second principle activity of the organization. If planning is the most neglected activity of organizations, developing is a close second. Developing is the process of ensuring that all team members have the skill to succeed at the task. A common misconception is that assignment to the team means you know what you are doing—as if being on the team imparted new, magical insights and abilities. Though a key *Fifth Station* tenet is that you already have most of what you need to succeed, you still *only* have most of what you need. Developing provides the incremental move forward that will produce outstanding results. Curiously, there is also an almost instinctive reluctance to develop people for the task at hand. When money gets tight, training is usually the first victim of the budgeteer's ax. This is more than just an issue of organizational budgets. Anyone who examines the crude tutorials that accompany today's sophisticated software will recognize that training just isn't a priority. In lieu of training, however, we get software that is tragically underutilized by operators who just don't know how to get the best results for their efforts.

One of the most common features of adult learners is their reluctance to admit that they don't know something. For this reason, the developing process should assess the skills needed for the project and then match those skills against a team member skill inventory. Before the project gets underway, all necessary training should be accomplished. Developing is an ongoing process. The skills necessary at the start of the project may not be the ones required in bringing it to completion. Additional and different training may be required. The developing process ensures that training is ongoing and provided when needed.

Developing includes skill acquisition, such as mastery of a new software program, but it includes professional development as well. To realize the benefits of balancing *sensing* with *intuition*, long duration teams should spend a part of every week expanding their knowledge of the task at hand as well as of information that might be only obliquely related to the immediate project. Some of the most innovative breakthroughs for a team will come from the fringes of their expertise. Examining information not directly related to the project is also a good way to keep the team sharp and avoid burnout. Developing is a transforming activity. It's a superb means of fostering team unity by providing a common, positive experience. It creates synergy by making the team greater than it originally was. On the subject, Mark Twain wrote, "Training is everything. The peach was once a bitter almond; cauliflower is nothing but cabbage with a college education."

Operating is the final activity. It's what the name suggests. Operating is the actual work done on the task. It's the *doing* phase of the project. It's the result of planning and developing. Despite our general zeal for just "doing it," operating will always be optimized by planning and developing. It is also the source for future planning and development activity. Feedback from the operating activity will shape concurrent planning and provide the information necessary to provide appropriate training. Operating is a powerful drive for us, but utterly dependent upon planning and developing for its effectiveness. The American sociologist, Charles Horton Cooley wrote, "We are born to action; and whatever is capable of suggesting and guiding action has power over us from the first." Planning and developing provide that power.

Planning, developing and *operating* reflect the order in the organizational chaos. They provide the structure for team activity. Each makes a distinct contribution toward achieving the goal, however, they are inextricably linked. In order to leverage their effectiveness, teams must isolate the activity. This reflects sensitivity to the basic simplicity of the structure. Effective teams will first know, "what they are doing." Secondly, effective teams will exercise balance between the three. The best results will come from the right application of planning, developing and operating. Finally, effective teams will never be far from WYSINWYG and the positive capacity for surprise. It will serve as a spur to find out what is happening when things seem most chaotic.

CONFIDENCE

It's 1933, and it couldn't get much worse. Almost 13 million wage earners—25% of the total work force—are unemployed. In some cities the figures are worse. In the northern industrial belt, Cleveland reports 50% unemployment; Akron 60% and Toledo an astounding 80% unemployment rate. Since 1929, ten thousand banks—40% of the 1929 total—have failed and depositors have lost over two billion dollars. Industrial stocks have lost 80% of their value since 1930. Farm income has declined by 60% and a third of all farms have been lost to their owners through mortgage foreclosures.

As if that isn't enough, the Midwest is gripped by a devastating drought. Summer temperatures soar above 100 degrees, swarms of grasshoppers fill the sky and choking dust storms roil across the fields and blot out the sun. Hundreds literally starve to death on city streets. Public and private relief agencies are crushed by the demand. Probably the best relief services are found in New York City, where families count themselves lucky if they receive the average $2.39 a week in aid.

But as bad as this is, it doesn't begin to describe the scope of the suffering experienced by most Americans, for the trouble began long before the crash in 1929. Today most people aren't aware that the "Roaring Twenties," only roared for a few. Despite a decade of strong growth, in 1929 more than half of all Americans lived below the minimum subsistence levels. The average annual per-capita income was a meager $750 and, incredibly, only $273 for farm families. The beleaguered farmer of the 30's had already seen farm values drop by 40% in the 20's. The massive bank failures of the early thirties had been preceded by an average of

600 failures a year in the twenties. While the richest one percent of Americans amassed 40% of the national wealth by 1929, the bottom 93% experienced a 4% drop in real disposable per-capita income over the same period.

By 1933 a deep despair had settled across the land and many people saw no hope for a better future. The economic depression spawned a psychological one, and large numbers of people, shamed by circumstance, literally never left home. And then things changed. In many ways, the man who brought about the change was an unlikely candidate. Wealthy, aristocratic and largely untouched by the Depression, he was a representative of the 1% rather than the 93%. And yet he had tenacity, charisma and incredible courage. Despite his personal wealth, he dedicated his entire adult life to public service. And he pursued that public service despite suffering from a crippling illness.

The man, of course, was Franklin Delano Roosevelt, 32nd President of the United States. FDR's inauguration on March 4, 1933 marked the fulcrum of the Depression. He assumed the presidency, pledging, "a New Deal for the American people," and though recovery would be slow, things would never be as bad again. Incredibly, spirits began rising rapidly with his election before a single New Deal policy or program could be put into place.

In his first inaugural address, FDR stated,

> This great Nation will endure as it has endured, will revive and will prosper. So, first of all, let me assert my firm belief that *the only thing we have to fear is fear itself*—nameless, unreasoning, unjustified terror, which paralyzes needed efforts to convert retreat into advance. In every dark hour of our national life a leadership of frankness and vigor has met with that understanding and support of the people themselves, which is essential to victory.

Most people reading these lines will *hear* Roosevelt as well. The Brahmin inflection and lilting cadence is a deeply familiar part of our national culture and his words are immediately recognizable to almost every citizen. The power behind the address, the transforming nature of this speech is found in Roosevelt's expression of confidence. In that first inaugural address, FDR expressed his ability to lead; in government's ability to effect positive change; and every American's ability to overcome adversity and to thrive. It was all about *confidence,* and confidence is where team *success* begins.

The wellspring of *confidence* is *belief.* When you believe in something, you accept and have conviction about the *truth, actuality,* or *validity* of that thing. When the belief is about you, its called *self-confidence.* Self-confidence is your belief that you can marshal your *physical, intellectual, emotional* and *spiritual* resources in the *successful* pursuit of a *goal.*

The number one predictor of individual or team success is confidence level. Confident people tend to initiate action and control their environment—even under difficult conditions. Your degree of self-confidence will determine the kinds of risks you take, the amount of effort you'll expend, and the strength of your perseverance in time of trouble. Your confidence will determine the amount of flexibility you creatively apply in new situations. Your confidence will promote either optimism or pessimism and will dictate the degree to which you are vulnerable to debilitating stress or depression.

Confidence is *intangible.* It is based upon your experience, but more importantly, on your *interpretation* of that experience. Most behaviors are governed by perceptions rather than by fact. Almost everyone has had the experience of watching someone perform well only to later find that the performer was disappointed with the results and was therefore downcast. This is often considered "snatching defeat from the jaws of victory." When the converse is true, we label the individual "clueless."

Whether hypercritical or clueless, an individual's perception of performance will largely determine future confidence levels. It's important to remember that confidence can't be bestowed. When we offer or receive support and encouragement, it is a way of shaping perception, but ultimately the individual alone determines their level of confidence.

Confidence, then, is your intangible belief in your ability to succeed. Typically, people apply their confidence in two different ways. The first is a *universal* application. Everyone has a base-line assumption about his or her ability. They know *generally* what they are good at and what they need help with. This cornerstone belief is your *universal self-confidence.* *Universal* confidence is a direct link to your training, education and experience. The sum total of this life experience provides a general framework against which you can assess your ability to succeed in a wide range of activities. It's your belief that you can handle life's vagaries with enough skill to maneuver successfully in virtually all settings that you consider routine.

An example of this is often seen when highly successful CEO's jump industries. They make the leap because they are confident that the skills necessary for managing people, assets and debt are largely consistent across industry lines. After all, you don't have to be a pilot to run an airline or a surgeon to run a hospital. Their high level of confidence encourages their belief that in any industry specific differences can be quickly mastered. Their past success easily generalizes to the new environment.

Situational confidence is the second application and reflects how you believe you will perform under a particular set of circumstances. It's not about your skills, but about how you think you can apply those skills in a specific and unique setting. It's a direct link to your past successes and failures. Because of this, your situational confidence will determine your willingness to accept or reject risk. The stronger your belief that you can succeed, the more likely you are to not only accept the risk, but to do so enthusiastically.

Individuals and teams that can accurately assess their situational confidence can easily avoid the unhappy discovery of finding themselves, "in over their heads." Getting in over your head is almost always the result of over-estimating the extent to which your abilities will generalize. A common example today is the "techie," who can build a better box, but who flounders as a marketer or CEO. The ultimate key to situational success is an accurate self-assessment and the *universal* confidence to heed it.

Both universal and situational confidence shares an intrinsic, vitalizing dynamic. The first part of that dynamic is that confidence *generalizes*. Experiencing success fosters confidence that generalizes to other, similar situations. This is the source of *universal* confidence. The second aspect of the dynamic is that confidence is *generative* as well. It creates the expectation of additional success. This, of course, is the source of *situational* confidence. As skills are applied to new situations in new ways, the experience of success generates a willingness to try new challenges, which, in turn, develop new and refine old skills. As new competencies are mastered, confidence grows and further generalizes. This *generative*, *generalizing* quality of confidence continually expands the range of experiences and environments in which you are willing to participate. Expecting to succeed increases motivation and actually results in improved performance. Even in the face of setbacks, the generative effect motivates by creating the expectation that new skills can be learned to overcome the immediate problem.

Confidence and Control

A good deal of *confidence* has to do with *control*. Control means you can influence the outcome of something. The absence of control is helplessness, the very opposite of confidence. Certainly, a major factor in Roosevelt's ability to inspire confidence was the fact that he actually *controlled* the executive branch of government and was in a position to actively shape legislation. Similarly, the old adage, "it is better to have loved and lost, than to never have loved at all," makes the point that even failure is preferable to never having had a chance to exercise *control* over your destiny. Control makes you a participant instead of a bystander—a player instead of a fan. To gain confidence, you *have* to be a player; you *have* to *know* that the results reflected *your* effort.

You can exercise control over people, things and yourself. Control of people and things is basically about task assignments and resource allocation. This is no mean feat. Success in either category is impressive and success in both the stuff of divinity. But this is the routine stuff of management. We know individuals and teams will demonstrate confidence by setting more challenging goals, working harder and having more resilience in the face of problems when they control their work and their resources.

Control over these aspects creates a sense of "ownership" and fosters pride that in turn builds universal confidence. Control need not be absolute in order to produce the desired effect. Collaborative relationships, management partnerships or shared governance of a project are all models that will build confidence as long as the individual recognizes that their influence is *real* and *integral* to the task. Control can't be faked. Individuals and teams without it will never come close to realizing their potential.

Control—rather, self-control—plays a far more significant role in relation to confidence building. In this context, self-control has nothing to do with not eating two desserts while on a diet or starting a long promised exercise program. Instead, it has to do with the extent to which an individual believes they can control their *ability*. One of the principle differences between those who maintain a high level of confidence and those who don't is the way in which they view *ability*.

Ability is the quality of being able *to do something*. It may be physical, intellectual, emotional or spiritual. Ability is qualitatively neutral. I may be *able* to sing, "Recondita armonia," from *Tosca*; but no one would accuse me of singing it *well*. Ability is often identified as natural or acquired. Natural ability implies a genetic endowment. It's an ability that came with birth and is there to be refined. Acquired ability is something you pick up along the way. Sparked by an interest or accident, a skill is worked and improved upon. Generally, people operate under the assumption that they have one type or the other. The two approaches, however, are fundamentally opposed and have a tremendous impact on confidence and, as a result, outcomes.

The belief that ability is *acquired* and can be continually enhanced through new learning and mastery, vigorously promotes confidence. People who hold this belief adopt goals that stretch their capabilities and offer the chance to perfect new skills. Challenges are understood as opportunities to gain knowledge. Errors and failures are recognized as common features of the learning process and are leveraged as learning opportunities rather than as demonstrations of personal deficiencies. Evaluation is on the basis of personal growth and development, rather than on the basis of individual comparisons. This view builds a resilient self-confidence. Such resilience helps people sustain their confidence in the face of severe adversity. It also challenges them toward new goals, and to effectively use their data-gathering and decision-making skills.

Those who view ability as *natural* believe that their performance reflects their innate intelligence. This produces strong concerns about self-esteem as errors and failures are understood as signs of personal weakness. These are powerful fears, which can actually impair decision-making ability. In response, people who hold this belief tend to pursue *pass/fail* goals in an effort to demonstrate competence. They will seek out tasks that highlight their proficiency in a setting that also minimizes the chance of failure.

Not surprisingly, they are less likely to seek out new learning because of the possibility of failure or looking foolish. They might also avoid new activities that would require high initial effort as such effort is often taken as a sign of low ability. Obviously, such people have difficulty managing failure. Frequent set backs erode their confidence. This, in turn, leads them to set lower goals that result in lower achievement. The negative generative effect weakens confidence, impairs judgment and reduces the possibility of success. Sadly, as problems increase, people with this belief tend to place blame on others and become increasingly critical.

WYSINWYG is ever active, so it is not surprising that both types initially appear very similar in confidence and organizational ability. The differences may only arise when faced with disappointing performance. Once again, those in the acquired skill group fare better. When confronted with poor performance, this group tends to become more focused and systematic in both data-gathering and decision-making. In a show of resilience, they continue to set challenging goals. In response to continued failure, their approach becomes even more systematic and with few strategy changes. When changes occur, they are applied systematically and made only on the basis of new data. The reason for this seems to be that members of this group don't feel betrayed by failure. Errors and mistakes are understood as the results of data or skill deficits. Address the deficit and the problem should go away. In this way problems are of interest in and of themselves, and also provide an opportunity to find novel resolutions.

Those who believe solely in natural ability tend to have problems as difficulties increase. Not surprisingly, their responses are in counterpoint to the previous group. A common response to setbacks is to frequently change strategies in an effort to find the best one. With successive failures the changes come more quickly and are applied erratically. This both confuses the team and limits the chance that any strategy will have sufficient opportunity for success. It also reduces the chance that enough data can be gathered to support a new plan. Oddly, people in this group might also behave in just the opposite manner, by sticking to a course of action that is failing, even in the face of contradicting information. It's the *Titanic Effect*, and a classic example of a confidence failure.

In either case, the problem resides with the *generative* anxiety produced by the failures and the consequent impaired decision-making ability. Decision-making is impaired because this group takes failure personally. At a time when they should be focusing on the problem at hand, their attention is diverted to personal second-guessing. They dwell on *their* failings rather than on the task. They begin seeking *personal feedback* instead of task related feedback. As their confidence erodes, they sense a loss of control and a developing helplessness. They ultimately come to view the task as harder than it actually is. As a result, they set lower goals and achieve less. Importantly, these people don't exert less effort. In fact, they work even harder to find the optimal solution. The difficulty is that their decision-making skills have become impaired, and with increasing activity they simply become more erratic in their applications.

Control is intrinsically related to confidence. It is powerfully active at both an operational level of controlling people and things, and at a psychological level of self-control. When control is absent or withheld, confidence erodes and helplessness and dependency emerge. Conversely, individuals and teams that exercise control are robust, resilient and successful.

Profile of Confidence

At this point, it may be helpful to identify the ten key indicators associated with confident individuals or teams. Keep in mind that these ten are landmark features of confidence. Because confidence is generative and generalizes, it is synergistic and has much in common with *chaos*. That is, there is a *sensitive dependence on initial conditions* at work. The indicators can combine in various patterns, with different emphasis, and produce different results. The key is recognizing and promoting the behavior you desire.

Ten Indicators of Confidence

1. Confident people (and teams) are *optimistic—they expect to succeed.*
2. They exercise *control* and accept *accountability* for themselves, their resources, and their work.

3. They set *challenging goals;* and as a result, accomplish more.

4. When confronted with problems, they are *resilient* and *persevering.*

5. They are *focused* data-gatherers and decision-makers.

6. They *systematically* initiate and implement change.

7. They continually *seek* out personal and team *development* opportunities.

8. *Failures* are recognized as a *routine part* of the *developing process.*

9. They base their *evaluations* on *development* and *operating goals.*

10. They make *celebration* an integral part of their operating style.

It's worth noting how many of these indicators relate to material we've already discussed in terms of *Chaos.* Of course, in the middle of the list are the two key functions of personality—data-gathering and decision-making. Since these two functions are at the heart of all human activity, it is not surprising that they should be major drivers of confidence. When we thoroughly gather data and make effective decisions (in our preferred type), we are definitely building confidence. Without success here, confidence would be continually eroded.

Note also how prominently the principle activities of the organization come into play. *Goal setting* is a key element of *planning.* As we will discuss in another chapter, the concept of systematic implementation, resilience, and perseverance all relate to effective goal setting and planning. No less than three of the indicators deal with *developing.*

As an organizational activity, developing bridges planning and operating. Here it is rooted to the recognition that ability can be *acquired* and as a consequence, confidence can be generated through new learning and skill mastery. Developing builds success by establishing a strong foundation for operating. Similarly, developing builds a foundation for confidence by enhancing the chance of success through new learning.

Finally, confidence is promoted by *evaluations* that measure operations, or the net result of your planning and developing. The *objective standards* required for successful operating can provide a clear picture of perform-ance. It's a picture, however, that stays focused on the task at hand. Confidence grows when we know the mark and can, thus, acknowledge success or identify the new developing that must take place as a response to failure.

WYSINWYG alerts us to the fact that more is usually going on than we can immediately apprehend. Chaos reminds us that there is a structure beneath all human operations. Paradigms and psychological type actively shape confidence. They provide the hidden structure that gives confidence its strength.

Having explored the basic indicators of confidence, it's worth a look at the indicators of helplessness. *Helplessness is the antithesis of confidence.* People without confidence slowly begin to lose the capacity to act. They become hesitant and then fearful. Numbed by indecision, they begin to look to others for all direction. This might work if there are other capable people to assist. Unfortunately, helplessness tends to be contagious and entire families; groups and nations can be afflicted. Roosevelt noted as much in his third inaugural address. Looking back he said, "Eight years ago, when the life of this Republic seemed frozen by a fatalistic terror, we proved that this is not true. We were in the midst of shock—but we acted. We acted quickly, boldly, decisively." Recognizing the signs of helplessness can provide the impetus for Roosevelt's quick, bold, decisive action.

Ten Indicators of Helplessness

1. *Pessimism*—the expectation that things won't go right.
2. An inward, personal focus that is *self-critical* and sees failures as a sign of weakness or deficiency.
3. *Critical of others* and *blaming* when things go wrong.

4. Exercises *limited control* with little accountability.

5. Sets *goals* that are *easily attainable* and thus, achieves less.

6. *Hesitant* data-gathering and decision-making: makes both easy and difficult tasks seem harder than they are; makes it difficult to spot available solutions.

7. *Avoids risks*: prefers performance goals with likelihood of success and avoids new learning or methods that may create appearance of low ability.

8. Works *harder*, but gets *fewer* results.

9. *Changes* strategies *frequently*: plans erratically; doesn't give an approach enough time to work before moving on.

10. *Resists* new information that contradicts original assumptions, master of the Titanic Effect.

The basis of helplessness is the failure to adequately develop the paradigms and type preferences that underlie confidence. Poor planning produces inferior goals. Planning weakness also fails to provide the measures to assess success or failure. Consequently, failure is easier to personalize. Resisting the concept of ability as an acquired skill leads to a reluctance for using developing as both a proactive and reactive tool. Actual operations are difficult to manage in the absence of clearly desired outcomes, making it easier to switch approaches. Again we can see that confidence and chaos are closely linked. Recognizing what is happening below the surface can avoid problems of helplessness altogether.

Promoting Confidence

We've already said that confidence is the single most important factor in determining an individual or team's likelihood of success. Promoting confidence is the first task that any leader should undertake. Even though confidence is a personal, intangible belief, it can be actively promoted. There are four basic ways to build confidence: the direct *experience* of success, (observing someone similar to you), *model* success, *coaching* (from a respected individual), and *celebration*.

The Experience of Success

The experience of success is unquestionably the best way to build confidence. Because confidence is *generative*, one success will encourage another. Because confidence *generalizes*, success in one area will promote confidence in other areas. Success, then, is the principle motivator for confidence. But what exactly is entailed in the direct experience of success? After all, everyone engages in scores of routine behaviors that might be technically classified as a success, but hardly seem to promote confidence.

The fact that you fixed the first pot of coffee in the office is hardly the stuff of heady exuberance and zeal to tackle new challenges. *That's because a behavior, once mastered, becomes routine and loses its power to motivate.* At one time, making a pot of coffee in the office that everyone didn't grouse about as being too strong or too weak probably produced a commensurate flicker of confidence. But once you got it down, you stopped thinking about it. It became just a routine part of the daily, blurry-eyed, early morning routine. In order to build confidence, the *success must be related to an objective that is valued and that holds the possibility for failure.* That is why making the big sale, or winning the difficult case, or diagnosing the obscure illness has such a powerful effect on us.

Success in the face of uncertainty motivates exponentially. It also sets the mark higher. The big sale becomes the biggest to date, the difficult case becomes part of your specialty, and the obscure diagnosis isn't as hard to spot the next time. This generative quality fosters future challenges. Success gives you the experience to confidently take on the next.

Direct experience, then, is the first way of promoting confidence. You have an objective, you apply your resources to attaining, it and you get the intrinsic high from your success. You know you did well and your confidence is intrinsically strengthened.

You can also find your confidence promoted by *feedback* regarding your success. When you first got the coffee right, you knew it because it tasted great and no one complained. You enjoyed a good cup of Joe and a quiet sense of confidence. That confidence, however, could be significantly strengthened by positive comments from your co-workers. Oblique compliments such as broad smiles, closed eyes, a contented, "ummmmmm," while the aroma was deeply inhaled, coupled with loud exclamations of, "this is terrific," might have you exploring coffeehouse franchises. *The simple act of receiving positive feedback on your performance synergistically increases the motivational impact.*

Whether salesman, lawyer or doctor, positive recognition helps build a resilient confidence. Importantly, this feedback does not have to be elaborate to be effective. Literal 'pats on the back,' and verbal, "attaboys," are usually all that are required. The *immediacy* of the feedback is important. Waiting six months until the Employee of the Year awards won't go nearly as far in promoting confidence.

There is a third way in which directly experiencing success can build confidence. This approach relies on the generalizing aspect of confidence. There are times when it is helpful to build confidence *before* taking on a specific objective. This can be done with case studies, simulations, team-building games and experiential exercises. In each case, the individual or team has a chance to succeed at something. That, "something," may be similar or only remotely associated to the ultimate task at hand. Pilots gain confidence by successfully handling crises in a simulator that could prove fatal if practiced in the air. Pilots can also gain confidence in their cockpit crew management skills by taking on high elements in an outdoors-experiential program. The value is that the direct experience of *associative* success is so motivating, that it can be productively generalized to confidence-building on the primary task.

It is worth saying again—the direct experience of success is the most important method of promoting confidence. Whether the successful experience is with the principle work objective, based on feedback about successful performance, or the result of success with an associative experience, it will powerfully build confidence in both the universal and specific realms. Confidence level is the best *predictor* of success, and the best way to build confidence is through the *experience* of success.

Modeling

Sometimes, before an individual can experience success, they have to learn how to do it. This brings us to the second method of promoting confidence, *modeling*. Modeling requires an actor and an observer. The actor is one who is confident and skilled in a particular behavior or activity. Fashion models, for example, are highly adept at making clothes look good. They know how to capture the spirit of an outfit and how to move in such a way that the clothing is displayed to its best advantage. Of course, in the process, the observer has a chance to evaluate the clothes. He or she mentally tries it on, and assesses if the result is sublime or ridiculous. The fact that one can do so without risking actually looking ridiculous is behind the power of modeling.

Modeling works because it *lowers an individual's anxiety about their ability* to accomplish something. When you observe the model, you learn the standard of performance and how the task is accomplished. You have a chance to measure your skills (specific confidence) against the model's, and *assess your chances for success*. This is how confidence is promoted through modeling. The model may simply confirm that you can do it, or you may see that more training will be required. Either way, you arrive at your decision in a relatively *risk-free* environment and have increased your confidence because you have a better idea of what will be required.

Sometimes the modeling relationship is *formal*. Often a rookie's first assignment is to shadow a seasoned professional. The rookie isn't along to do anything other than soak up the experience. Of course, even a rookie knows the dangers inherent in brewing a *bad* pot of coffee first thing in the morning. Observing an old pro handle the scoop, filter, and water lets the new kid learn the system without incurring the wrath of the vets. The rookie can gain confidence by learning the ropes in a virtually no-risk environment.

Of course many modeling relationships are entirely *informal*. What parents often identify as negative peer pressure is actually their child modeling the values displayed in the home. Both kids and adults regularly model the behavior and fashions found in the movies or on television. This modeling is often unconscious, but it points to how common it is in our society. Adopting the style of a particular athlete or actor boosts confidence because the observer has seen how others positively relate to the super star. The *generalizing* assumption is that, "if it works for the rich and famous, it will work for me." Sadly, informal modeling usually produces hit or miss results.

Many a parent has lamented that their children seem only to have acquired their *bad* habits. This has cautionary overtones in the workplace. Leaders should pay close attention to their organizational culture. As new members come on board, they will ultimately end up modeling the actual behavior of the environment. If the environment reflects your mission, vision and values, so much the better. However, if there is a mismatch between what you say and what you do, most people will follow the action. Actions *do* speak louder than words when it comes to modeling.

Formal modeling, however, is an ideal way of building confidence. If done with a clear end in mind, it can provide a solid foundation for someone to experience success by preparing him or her to do so. It will give them the confidence to try something that they may have been reluctant to do before.

Coaching

The third method of building confidence is *coaching*. Like modeling, coaching helps get someone ready to directly experience success. The coach provides explicit direction and support. It's a *persuasive relationship* that in the end will convince you that you can succeed on your own. In many ways coaching is a hybrid between the action of experiencing a thing and the observation associated with modeling. To be effective, the coach must be *credible*. That is, he must be knowledgeable about the subject and have had successful experience with it. Returning to our office coffeepot for a moment, we can see the effects of successful coaching. The seasoned office coffee maker will coach the new employee, not by making the coffee for him, but by making helpful suggestions. Things like, "*never use tap water—get water from the cooler*," and, "*careful now, level scoops—not rounded*," and for the truly advanced, "*its all in the timing and the wrist—you have to laterally rotate to get the pot back on the burner before coffee spills everywhere*."

Unlike the model, the coach doesn't necessarily engage in the activity, but stands aside and persuades a participant/observer that *they* can do it. The coach's favorite expression is, "*you* try it!" The best coaches will be hands on. They can *demonstrate* as well as critique. The most important aspect of good coaching, however, is the *relationship between the coach and the coached*.

The coaching situation sacrifices some of the risk-free aspects of modeling. Though still not on your own, in a coaching relationship you have to put it on the line. The "it" is your fledgling confidence because there is a likelihood you'll fail before you get it right. The coaching relationship is one that tolerates failure, but human egos being what they are, nobody wants to appear foolish or inept under *any* circumstances. It's up to the coach to ensure that your performance receives enough support so that even when you miss the mark, it incrementally builds your confidence that you can ultimately succeed.

A coaching relationship is usually *time specific*. The coach is engaged to bring you to a specific point. Once you've reached that point the relationship ends. You begin to build confidence by actually doing the "thing." You may, however, elect to reengage the coach. Coaches can help you move to the next level of achievement or help you find a new coach more attuned to your new needs. The relationship also ends if you lose confidence in the coach. If the coach is no longer credible—for whatever reason—the relationship won't be productive. Nothing is gained by staying in a coaching relationship that you've outgrown or don't trust.

There are many levels of coaching. At one end of the spectrum you'll find intense, one-on-one coaching such as that provided by personal trainers. The critique is entirely focused on you and the pursuit of your very specific goals. In the middle of the spectrum are situations in which you may function as the "junior partner," for a project. In this case you learn, not only from observation, but also by doing tasks of moderate complexity under the guidance of seasoned workers. At the other end of the spectrum are informal mentoring relationships in which someone who knows the ropes at levels above you helps you along. These relationships can be formal, but often are spontaneous as well, and rooted in office collegiality.

Celebration

The final way of building confidence is an altogether different, but no less powerful approach. It is probably the most neglected means of promoting confidence and also the one that produces the most lasting results. Before continuing, however, a brief digression is in order. As we've been discussing coffee at some length, it might be helpful to now consider *tea*.

The British are renown for their tea drinking. For them, it seems to serve as a national all-purpose drink. They drink it at home, at work, morning, noon and night. Despite the frenetic drinking, tea is probably more a cultural comfort beverage than anything else. At the first sight of any problem someone is immediately dispatched to brew a "cuppa." Any avid follower of BBC and Granada television programs knows this to be case. In fact, the alacrity with which junior constables appear to produce tea at crime scenes leaves one certain that it's a part of their formal training.

Less well known is the vast amount of tea drinking that goes on in the Mideast. It is common in the Arab world to precede all business transactions with a cup of tea. Many times, one cup won't do and numerous cupfuls are swallowed in an effort to get almost anything done. In these countries, tea drinking assumes a formal air. It's as much a part of the business routine as shaking hands is here. It's how business is *done*.

No one though, can best the Japanese when it comes to tea drinking. Since its introduction over 1,000 years ago, *cha-no-yu,* or, tea ceremony, has become an integral part of the Japanese cultural landscape. Originally used to aid meditation, tea drinking was gradually elevated to an art form through the application of Zen and the spiritual discipline of the samurai. The increasingly ritualized ceremony was designed to foster serenity in the midst of turbulent times.

Those fortunate enough to attend a tea ceremony today will find that it combines art, ritual and mediation in a remarkably holistic orchestration. Each utensil in the ceremony is considered a unique work of art and is introduced singly to those in attendance. Just one bowl of tea is prepared at a time and is consumed only after the cup has been carefully admired. The tea itself is consumed in three gulps interspersed with meditative pauses. More than a beverage, tea drinking has come to symbolize tranquility, hospitality and comfort.

By now you're probably ready for a cup of tea and an explanation of what this has to do with confidence. Consider: the British routinely use tea for comfort and the Arabs routinely use tea as an instrument of business, but the Japanese *celebrate* with tea. Because the ceremony is deliberate and slow, it breaks the rhythm of daily routine. It also has a commemorative, distinctive quality. The act of ceremony is noteworthy and not easily forgotten. Very significantly *cha-no-yu* is WYSINWYG and symbolizes much more than what it appears to be.

When we apply these aspects of celebration to our successes, we are creating a motivating force that is entirely *disproportionate to the initial experience*. A personal or team success, when celebrated, unleashes a long-lasting positive effect. Morale, productivity, effectiveness and quality all increase in response to a celebration. Best of all, the celebration need not be elaborate to create the effect. It can be as simple as a team picnic during a regular lunch break, or a potluck breakfast preceding a staff meeting. The essential elements are only that the *success be recognized with credit given where do, and that it occurs in close proximity to the experience.*

We've already seen that feedback is a primary means of promoting confidence. The celebration is basically an advance on the pat on the back. It tells someone that they've done well, and it also alerts a larger group of people to the success. In this way, the celebration becomes a well-known benchmark of success. *The act of commemorating a success becomes a successful experience in and of itself.* The public recognition greatly enhances the confidence of the individual or team while providing an associative boost of confidence to those on the periphery of the experience.

This form of public celebration has a collateral value as well. Celebration permits others only tangentially involved to derive benefit from the success. This is known as *basking in reflected glory*. This occurs when you share the success of others *by identification rather than by participation*. People are attracted to success and want to be identified with it. They want to work for prestigious companies, report to the most successful leaders and work on the best teams. They want to become a part of the successful reputation. Those standing in the reflected glory actually gain in confidence by being *associated* with a winning team, be it sports, work or home related. The power of celebration is that it produces synergy for the direct participants and has a generative and generalizing effect on others as well. Confidence is boosted throughout the organization as the ripples are experienced and interpreted by others. The effect is powerful and, importantly, it can be created with simple planning.

An interesting corollary to this effect is that while celebrating success increases overall confidence, *commemorating a failure can reduce its negative impact*. If the failure is understood as an opportunity for learning and has resulted from a good faith effort, the act of commemoration can have a positive and consoling effect. Thus, taking note of a failure might actually boost confidence as the problem is openly confronted, evaluated and the positive effort noted. In both good times and bad, celebration fosters hope.

The four ways of promoting confidence can work alone or in concert, but important point to remember is that confidence is the single greatest key to success. Confidence can be home grown and nurtured, thus, it's vital that individuals and teams be provided the opportunity to succeed as part of their development, either by assigning progressively more difficult tasks or by scheduling associative experiences. High-energy models or coaches can be employed.

However it's done, this is a function of the planning process. The best results will come from the best-developed resources. It's also a planning function to ensure that success, and sometimes failure, is celebrated on a routine basis. That is not to say that the celebration should become routine—celebrating Tuesdays would quickly lose its impact—but it should be recognized as an integral part of the work process. Growing confident people and teams is the primary leadership responsibility.

Expecting to Succeed

We started this discussion with the Depression, and it may be helpful to return there now. Many of the banks failed because they were insolvent. It was a time of little regulation, no insured deposits and no guarantees about the skill of the bankers. It was a heyday for mismanagement and corruption. But curiously, a large number of solvent and well-managed banks failed as well. The problem was that people had come to *expect* bank failures. Thus, when they heard a rumor that *their* bank was insolvent, they dropped everything and raced to get their money out. This became a literal *run* on the bank. Of course as depositors panicked, it fueled and gave credence to the initial rumor. More panic ensued and in the frantic withdrawal scramble, the bank was actually pushed into insolvency. This is why one of Roosevelt's first acts was to declare a bank holiday. It stopped the bank runs and provided a much needed cooling off period. What was truly amazing was that the simple *expectation of an event actually caused it to happen.*

This phenomenon is called the *self-fulfilling prophecy.* We've already seen how this is active in the growth of self-confidence. Your *universal* sense of confidence equips you to take on any number of challenges with the *expectation* of success. Your success in *specific* cases generalizes and fuels your motivation to succeed in other similar cases. In this way, your *expectation* of success becomes a self-fulfilled prophecy as you identify a goal and then attain it. In effect, you live up to your own press.

But there is more. While studying the dynamics of the self-fulfilling prophecy, researchers uncovered a fascinating corollary. Rosenthal and Jacobson first described it in their 1968 landmark study, *Pygmalion in the Classroom.* In the study, a group of randomly selected teachers were told that certain of their students had demonstrated particularly high potential for academic growth on the basis of a standardized test. In reality, there was no difference between these students and those in a control group. Yet at the end of the year, a very clear difference emerged. Those students, whom the teachers had *expected* to excel, did in fact do so. On the basis of standard tests given to all students at the end of the year, those identified as high potential actually scored higher than the control group. It was clearly a case in which the expectation of others produced positive results in the target individual. This has come to be called the *Pygmalion Effect.*

In Roman mythology, Pygmalion was both a king and a misogynist. Dissatisfied with the quality of females in general, he carved a statue of the ideal woman. Pygmalion became so enamored with his own work that he prayed to Venus to bring the statue, Galatea, to life. Venus generously obliged and many wonderful things transpired, not the least of which is that he was he was cured of his misogyny. His name is given to the Pygmalion Effect because the transformation of the inanimate into the living is indicative of the awesome power of setting high standards and expecting them to be fulfilled for others.

The Pygmalion Effect works very simply. It begins with a respected, *credible* authority—teacher, parent, leader, manager—communicating *high expectations* to the target individual or team. The targeted individual *internalizes* the expectation and *behaves* accordingly. In essence, an authority is expressing confidence in your ability and in response you *act* confidently. In turn, the authority responds to your confident behavior by providing more constructive feedback and setting more challenging goals. The net result is that you achieve more because more has been levied and both you and the authority expect success.

The simplicity of the Pygmalion process shouldn't be underestimated. Productivity gains ranging between 10% and 30% have been recorded strictly on the basis of leader expectations. Certainly, with these kinds of gains possible, the Pygmalion process should be actively employed. In our discussion on building confidence, we noted that the single most effective means of promoting confidence was through the actual experience of success. At that point we indicated that specific, individual successes would synergistically motivate a person or team. This is a cumulative approach to confidence building. The Pygmalion process, in contrast, suggests that the actual architecture of the team include the experience of success. The goal is to create and manage an environment that is conducive to *growing* confident teams. There are five basic ingredients for this kind of growth.

First, the leader must have an *accurate idea of the team's capabilities*. The accuracy of the assessment will permit the formulation of performance standards and goals that stretch the team without setting them up for failure. It is amazing how little most leaders and managers really know about their personnel. The views are often extremely narrow and consequently limit the team's potential. Leaders prior to any consideration of team goals should actively engage the principle of WYSINWYG, assessing a full and well-rounded picture of the team before doing anything else.

Secondly, once you've formulated your expectations, *communicate* them fully to the team. Don't hedge. Make sure they recognize the stretch while lavishing praise about their high potential. It's important that you are clear; the clarity of your expectations will directly impact the likelihood of success. It's also important that everyone knows why the other guy is on the team. You've selected people for good reasons, though these may not be transparent to everyone else. People aren't always willing to toot their own horn, so the leader should do it for them.

Thirdly, provide *routine, constructive feedback*. Don't wait for milestones. Remember that we noted that immediate, small-scale feedback is usually more motivating than single instances of formal recognition that occur long after the noteworthy event. Frequent pats on the back, compliments and public recognition in routine meetings are essential for high-energy teams. *Listening* is also critical. Give the team frequent opportunities to *tell* you about what's happening. Again, these occasions are not formal, milestone reports, but informal chances to share thoughts.

Of course, none of this should be done insincerely. Insincerity is de-motivating and easily spotted. Feedback should always be high quality. It should be *constructive rather than critical*. That is, it should *celebrate* what's right and *coach* what's wrong.

Fourth, stay attuned to team successes and *increase the challenge when the stretch goes slack*. Successful teams routinely exceed expectations. They also thrive on challenge. As team confidence grows through successful accomplishment, its capability increases. Nothing will dull a good team faster than the status quo. WYSINWYG is always active. As teams change, so should their expectations. Recognize excellence by matching new goals with increased team capability.

Finally, *publicize*. Make sure that your *plan* for the project includes as much publicity for the team as possible. As has already been noted, public recognition produces long lasting motivational effects. To the extent appropriate for the project, the team should be recognized routinely and through a variety of media. This can cover the full range from news releases and articles in the house organ, to promotional items or distinctive clothing. The key is that the recognition is *regular* and *positive*.

The Pygmalion process is a self-consciously applied means of designing team cultures that foster confidence. It's simple, direct and capable of producing dramatic improvements in productivity and achievement at virtually no cost. An environment that maximizes the experience of success for each individual exponentially increases the probability of project success.

Confidence

Again, *confidence* makes the difference. Confidence will permit you to comfortably manage the routine while propelling you to new challenges and opportunities. It will expand your vistas. It will produce perseverance in the face of obstacles, and promote ingenious problem-solving strategies. It is the resilient source of individual and group resolve, not to be defeated by circumstances. It is the foundation of all successful teams. It *is* the Fifth Station.

STATION TEAMS

Henry Ford produced his first Model T in 1908. This would be "a motor car for the great multitude." Yet at $950 it remained far out of reach for most Americans. But Ford had an idea. After studying other industries (including Chicago's meat packing plants and a grain elevator) he and his team found a way to bring extreme efficiency to the manufacture of automobiles. Reflecting on the process in a 1926 essay, Ford commented, "the key word to mass production is simplicity. Three plain principles underlie it: (a) the planned orderly progression of the commodity through the shop; (b) the delivery of work instead of leaving it to the workman's initiative to find it; (c) an analysis of operations into their constituent parts. These are distinct but not separate steps; all are involved in the first one."

Though the principles were plain, implementation proved elusive. It took five years of tinkering, testing and study for Ford and his team to work out the details. Then in 1913, the principles became operational and the world's first moving assembly line for large-scale manufacturing began producing Model T's.

Ford's assembly line made everyone a winner. By 1914 the Highland Park, Michigan plant was turning out a completed chassis every 93 minutes—an astounding 635 minutes less than the previous average. Simultaneously, Ford cut the workday from nine to eight hours. The cut meant he could operate three shifts a day and ultimately produce a Model T every 24 seconds. This manufacturing revolution would ultimately be responsible for a $280 drop in the sticker price.

But Ford was more than just a production man. He recognized that increased volume without an increased market was simply a recipe for bankruptcy. Again, in his 1926 essay, he commented, "The experience of the Ford Motor Co. has been that mass production precedes mass consumption and makes it possible, by reducing costs and thus permitting both greater use-convenience and price-convenience. If the production is increased, costs can be reduced. If production is increased 500%, costs may be cut 50%, and this decrease in cost, with its accompanying decrease in selling price, will probably multiply by 10 the number of people who can conveniently buy the product. This is a conservative illustration of production serving as the cause of demand instead of the effect...."

Determined to make Ford workers, Ford consumers, he doubled salaries to $5 a week. Despite howls of protest from other industrialists, Ford stood by his decision and was rewarded by the sight of his assembly line workers purchasing Model T's of their own. Before it was all over in 1927, Ford had manufactured 15,000,000 Model T's and forever changed the American landscape.

Mass production coupled with mass consumption turned the automobile from a luxury to a necessity. It provided easy mobility and freed rural Americans from the confines of their small communities. It transformed the cities by making the suburbs possible, and the nation, by making an interstate highway system inevitable. And, it should come as no surprise, that it also provided a compelling illustration of how *teams* should be assembled.

Consider the assembly line: it relies on continuous and orderly flow, it maximizes worker productivity by providing work when and where it's needed, and it relies on the careful arrangement of constituent parts. Through its organization, the assembly line leaves little to chance. Successful teams, as well, leave little to chance. They are *assembled* in ways that maximize team member productivity. Their structure optimizes the continuous flow of data for decision-making, and their discrete parts are finely tooled to facilitate the entire process.

Too often teams aren't assembled. They just happen. A project comes along and a team is assigned to work it. The group gathers and attempts to figure out a solution, but trouble begins brewing almost at once. Only some of the people do any work. Some people don't get along. Meetings are frequent and mind numbing. No one is quite sure what the assignment actually *is*.

Underlying these problems is confusion about the nature of teams themselves. The world seems to have gone mad for teams, but what are they anyway? The answer isn't very complicated. *Teams are organizations in which two or more individuals work together to complete a task.* Implicit is the sense that everyone on the team is on the same side. Everybody is working together. Beyond this simple definition lies an astounding array of teams. They come in all sizes and complexities. They conduct dizzying numbers of meetings and are assigned innumerable tasks. With corporate America's discovery of multi-disciplinary teams, the size and number of teams has mushroomed. Cross-departmental teams ranging in size from 15 to 30 members are common in a mad rush to be sure that every possible specialty connected with a product is represented. Sadly, things are getting far more complicated than they need to be.

The misuse of teams is rooted in the *myth of team effectiveness.* Teams are put together in the commonplace belief that, "two heads are better than one." This is true to some extent. A team brings more data and a broader perspective to any project, however, casually assembled and chartered teams are notoriously inefficient. Their most significant weakness is their *inability to draw out all the valuable information available* within the team.

Another major problem is that unless carefully organized to do so, teams *rarely make full use of their allotted time.* It's a problem of, "so little time, so many distractions." Since people are social creatures, they enjoy working with others more than working alone. The team meeting is a social forum that in addition to actual task-related work serves to sustain the organizational culture. Even with good leadership, it is very easy for teams to drift off topic and simply socialize. Without fully realizing it, vast quantities of time can be lost to non-productive, albeit, pleasant conversations.

Ironically, another team weakness is the fact that there is safety in numbers. Because poorly assembled teams tend to diffuse accountability, some people feel more comfortable working in a group where they are unlikely to be singled out for anything—either good *or* bad. This attitude can promote behavior that actually blocks productivity.

Probably the most serious aspect of the myth is the belief that by simply assembling people on a team a better outcome will result. The entire team concept is centered on the belief that a team can accomplish more than an individual working alone. But based on our knowledge of teams, we know this is an inaccurate assumption. The real issue is whether the team is more effective when each member works alone rather than when working together. As we will see, the team is a highly effective instrument, but only when appropriately assembled.

Well-assembled teams are called *Station Teams*. Station teams are based on what we know to be true about people and organizations and are aligned with the principles of WYSINWYG, balance and simplicity. The constituent parts of station team assembly are size, civics, and work. Each of the parts is important in its own right, but taken together, they provide for continuous and effective team operation. Their assembly optimizes the chances for success.

Station Team Size and Productivity

When it comes to teams, size does matter. By definition it takes at least two people to make a team—there is no upper limit. But studies have consistently shown that *performance is directly related to team size*. With over forty years of research supporting the contention, we know that team size *optimizes* at *five* members. Beyond this point, productivity *plateaus* between six and nine members. With more than nine members there is a distinct productivity *loss*. The implication is obvious—keep teams small.

Part of the size problem is social. As teams increase in size, roles multiply and rules of engagement become more complicated. It becomes harder to involve everyone in the data-gathering or decision-making process. The result is a loss of effectiveness and plummeting productivity. Large teams can waste upwards of 30% of their time arguing about agendas, time limits, role assignments and the like. The bottom line is that big teams cost more—often a lot more—and deliver less. Five members are an ideal size for most projects.

Interestingly, when size expands beyond five members, teams employ a natural corrective. The corrective is to form *operational teams* within the larger team. The *operational team* is the smaller, core group that does most of the work. The operational team usually organizes informally. Without being asked, the core group simply begins assuming more responsibility. Those on the periphery, again informally, step aside and let the others do the work. This is such a common phenomenon that it's amazing leaders still insist on forming huge teams.

But the phenomenon is no secret to team members. Every member has a pretty clear understanding of who is doing the work (a small group), who is doing some work (a larger group), who just comes to meetings (closing in on the whole group now), and whose names go on the final product (everyone's). While increasing costs, there is *no benefit associated with large teams.*

But small teams don't necessarily imply limited input. Researchers have known for decades that *the pooled information of individuals working alone far exceeds the quantity and quality of information gathered by a team working face-to-face.* The most common experiment used to study this dynamic involves contrasting the performance of a four-member team with the pooled results of four individuals working on the same problem. The pooled results routinely exceed the team results by nearly 100%.

It is clear, that despite popular perception, teams actually inhibit goal-directed creativity. Size is a factor here as well. While team productivity optimizes at five members before it plateaus and then declines, there is no corresponding effect with pooled member productivity. In fact, in one study on creative problem solving, nine individuals working alone and then pooling their data produced 400% more ideas than a nine-member team that worked the problem face-to-face. It's worth noting, too, that the nine member face-to-face team produced no more than a five member face-to-face team in this experiment.

The data on team size and productivity suggests that the best teams will have a *two-tiered organization*. The *first tier,* or *core* team, will be made up of roughly five people who are tasked with project completion. They exercise control over the project's management and are accountable for the outcome. The core team is supported, in turn, by the *second tier,* or *associates,* who provide additional data and insight. The size of the associate group is limited only by the core team's requirements for data. The core team is tasked with requesting, pooling and analyzing the associate's input.

Balance and simplicity are particularly important here. The two-tiered system allows teams to balance the skills required to bring a project to completion, with the need to have access to as much data as possible. The associates can provide that balance. They can be used for specific issues or on a rolling basis. But they should only be used to balance the core. Too many associates could produce information overload that could confuse the core team's focus. Things should also be kept simple. Large meetings of associates are probably unnecessary. Their contribution is based not only on their skills, but also on the fact that individuals working alone can produce more and better data face-to-face teams on some problems. Systems for accessing associates and pooling their data should be kept lean.

Roles

Our discussion of core and associate station team members raises the related issue of *roles*. This is certainly an area in which complexity often reigns. Some programs recommend *six separate roles per team* (leader, scribe, timekeeper, process guide, facilitator and member). The first clue that this is overdoing it comes with the awareness that optimal team size is only five members. Some of the problem is the confusion of roles and responsibilities. Your *role* on the team describes your *broad function*. It reflects all the behaviors expected of you in that capacity and expresses your relationship to those with other roles. *Responsibilities* are the *specific obligations* that go along with a role. Responsibilities can be delegated. For example, record keeping is a responsibility of someone in a leadership role. The record keeping can be delegated, but that does not relieve the leader of accountability for the accuracy of the records.

In the spirit of simplicity, there are only three roles associated with station teams: team maker, team leader and team member. The *team maker* is the individual who decides that a team should address a particular issue. She's the person with work to be done. This individual is the driving force behind the team. She will determine initial goals, membership, do all the necessary pre-planning and coordinate development. She'll be responsible for orientation to both the team and the task. She'll set the goals and determine the rewards. Most often, the team maker will be external to the team, but this is not always the case. In either event she'll broker resources beyond the capability of the team itself and champion the team to the organization's hierarchy. Recalling our discussion of chaos, the team maker's *chief responsibility is planning and development*. Even in situations where the team maker ends up on the team, the preparatory planning and development must be accomplished. Team assembly is a team maker responsibility.

The second station team role is *team leader*. The leader exercises operational control and responsibility. Leaders must be chosen not only on the basis of their subject matter competency, but also on the strength of their human relations skills and organizational savvy. The leader's first responsibility is to establish and maintain focus. Once the goal is assigned, the leader is responsible for ensuring that all activity is directed toward achieving the objective. This includes responsibility for concurrent planning, satisfying training needs and facilitating the operating needs of the team. The leader ensures evaluation is ongoing. The leader is the primary confidence builder and ensures that celebration is an integral part of the team's activity.

The leader is also the team logistician. She is responsible for all the details of the team's management, recording and circulating information, agendas, meeting times and locations, coordinating content resources, provision of supplies and equipment, publicity and up-line reporting. To be sure, tasks can be shared or delegated, but the leader is ultimately both responsible and accountable.

In some ways, team leadership is a thankless burden. The only power associated with the role is that which is inherent in managing an organization. When it comes to decision-making, the leader is simply the "first among equals." That is, she has no more decision-making authority than anyone else does. She's not the boss, tiebreaker, final word or ultimate authority. She'll facilitate discussion and mediate dissent, but never force an edict. Should the team reach an impasse, the team maker intervenes to resolve the dispute. Of course, station teams are unlikely candidates for an impasse because of the team maker's careful up front investment in planning and developing.

The third role is the *team member*. In a speech made early in his presidency, Teddy Roosevelt said, "The first obligation of every citizen in this republic of ours, is that he pull his own weight." "Pulling their own weight," is the first responsibility of team members. Team members are involved in operations. They are the ones who will make the project happen. If the goal is to be achieved, it will be because the team members succeeded. It's essential that they demonstrate initiative, motivation and a willingness to take responsibility for their own participation.

Team members are chosen for the skills and knowledge that they can directly apply to the project. Not only are they content experts, but also must have facility with team building and interpersonal skills. Members can be expected to fulfill many delegated roles and temporary assignments, but their primary focus will always be on goal attainment.

They will work *collegially* with the leader. Members are expected to constantly push their knowledge envelopes and provide new ideas and input. They should recognize a need and fill it—never sit back and wait for the leader to "serve." Team members who find that they cannot participate must demonstrate the courage to simply resign. Station teams are deliberately small and one member, who is not "on board," cuts productivity by 20%.

There are two other categories of team members. The first is the *associate member*. We've already seen that associates function as team multipliers. They can expand the capability of the team without the loss of productivity found on large teams. Associates are essentially *independent consultants*. They may simply submit information as part of a pooling effort, or join the team for anywhere from a few hours to several weeks. The distinction is that the skill they bring to the team is not necessary for the duration of the project.

There is often a tendency to expand the core team by incorporating associates in frequent face-to-face meetings. This is almost always a mistake. The best use of the associate is as an independent source of pooled data. Associates should come and then they should go. They multiply the capability of the core team without supplanting it.

That said, associates shouldn't be considered as junior partners. The associate role is different than that of a core member only in *degree*. Team makers and leaders should be certain that the position is understood as a formal, accountable assignment. Associate members must understand the goal as clearly as core members. They *may* require development prior to participation. They *will* require feedback and a share of the recognition.

A final category of team member is *support* staff. On teams that will meet for extended periods of time, or for which tasks are particularly complex, a support team member can be a valuable addition. The support member does just that. He supports the efforts of the team by providing a wide range of logistical assistance that would otherwise be completed by the members themselves. This includes everything from gathering supplies, to publishing agendas, to coordinating the participation of associate members.

A support member might also be used to provide team building or facilitation expertise if the team is struggling with such issues. The distinction here is that a support member's duties are *adjunct* to those of the core team. The support member helps maintain team focus by attending to activity collateral to the primary goal of the team. They make logistical things happen so that team members don't have to worry about them, and then they stay discreetly out of the way.

The First Stop on the Assembly Line

Size is the first stop on the station team assembly line. Keep the following points in mind when assembling a team:

1. Smaller is better—no more than five to seven core members
2. Multiply the small team's capability through second tier associates
3. Assign only three roles: team maker, team leader, and team members.

Team Civics

The ancient Romans called those who lived beyond the Empire's boundaries, "barbarians." The word itself was demeaning. It suggested that non-Romans didn't have a language, but bleated like animals: "bar, bar." The term also implied a lack of civility. The Roman's most prized possession was citizenship. Notions of civility and citizenship were bound up in the concept of city living. Roman's lived in cities, and thus, were civilized. Barbarians were nomadic or rural, and consequently, uncivilized. Without pushing the illustration too far, the Roman concept was that city living required the development and exercise of social skills. They believed that city life would be unbearable in the absence of some code of conduct. In fact, the survival of the entire empire hinged on the harmonious and productive functioning of its many peoples. Civility was what Rome had to offer the world.

Teams, like the Roman Empire, require the use of social skills. A team is primarily a social unit, and as such requires liberal applications of civility in order to thrive. This entails demonstrating respect for others, exercising courtesy and acting politely. It means behaving with integrity and putting the needs of the many above your own. When exercised, civility grows strong teams that are highly resilient. It produces long lasting loyalties, builds confidence and super charges productivity. Nothing, however, undermines a team faster than a lack of civility among its members. Such a lack has a devastating and corrosive effect. It must never be permitted to take root.

People usually know what is socially required. They enjoy being treated well and consequently know how to treat others. Because civility is discretionary, it rarely has formal status in the work place. To be sure, most employers have policies regarding employee conduct, but few of these deals with subjects such as being *"nice"* to one another. Yet, being "nice" is one of those low cost, high payback behaviors.

Well-assembled teams actively promote civics and address both the personal and professional aspects of civility. *Personal civility* comes closest to simply being nice. It includes all the pleasant lessons we've learned from our childhood. It's the "thank you," and, "please," sort of behavior that parents instill. Personal civility fosters good fellowship. It makes you feel valued and glad to be on the team. *Professional civility* includes those behaviors that we agree are essential in environments where opinions might vary but decisions must be made none-the-less. These behaviors are the ones that help us gather and objectively analyze data. They provide the social mechanisms that permit us to navigate subjective subjects, such as personal values and beliefs, without resorting to violence. While most of these behaviors are self-evident, a quick look might help clarify what teams should encourage.

Personal civility is simply a matter of being considerate. You demonstrate it when you:

- Speak positively about other members and the organization
- Treat everyone with dignity, courtesy, and respect
- Accept problems with good nature
- Do something nice for someone else
- Bring treats without being asked
- Organize team celebrations, lunch time pot lucks, or picnics
- Defend the team and members from unfair criticism
- Assume good will
- Help others catch up if absent
- Greet everyone in the morning and say goodbye at night
- Plan social activities so that everyone is included
- Remember birthdays
- If invited to do so, show interest in other members' personal lives
- Offer frequent praise and constructive feedback
- Phone in if running late

Professional civility is demonstrated when you:
- Actively keep everyone informed
- Listen carefully
- Bring yourself up to date when you fall behind
- Refuse to play politics
- Practice integrity—do what you say you'll do
- Represent your point of view honestly

- Ban sarcasm, complaining, belittling, or blaming
- State opinions as opinions and not as facts
- Actively promote the free exchange of ideas
- Meet deadlines
- Manage time well
- Seek information and suspend judgment until facts are in
- Arrive on time and prepared
- Help others succeed
- Give credit where it's due

We learned a good deal about civil behavior on the steep slopes of Mt. Fuji. Tourist literature on Fuji often mentioned the small "hotels" that could be found at many of the stations. It was suggested that these hotels made for ideal resting places. Some actually took reservations.

The reality was somewhat different. The hotels were crude cabins warmed by open fires. Cold and wet, our group stopped at one, and after paying the tariff, was led to a large double-decked pallet. There we were placed on our sides, head-to-toe and covered with a large, damp quilt. As other unfortunate climbers sought refuge from the ice storm outside, the quilt was simply peeled back and the new arrivals added—sardine like—to the pallets.

Smoke burned our eyes, damp chilled our bones and the accumulated smells of dozens of marinating climbers created an atmosphere all its own. No one, however, complained. Instead, everyone made the best of it. There was quiet laughter (so as not to disturb those who could actually sleep), whispered words of encouragement and an instant rapport with strangers.

There was nothing complicated about what was going on at that time. By one accord, we were all behaving considerately—civilly—and the result was emotional warmth that drove out any discomfort. That is the power of civil behavior. It produces positive effects that are disproportionate to the effort expended.

We've listed just a few of the many behaviors that promote team civility. Though they seem obvious, many teams neglect them through lack of attention.

The single best way for civility to become an inherent part of the team's operation is to discuss it. In the station team assembly process, establishing high standards of civility falls to the leader. It should be the subject of one of the first team meetings and agreement on standards should be one of the team's first decisions. It never hurts to actually write down the agreed upon standards and distribute them to everyone. These written standards become the team's *protocol* for dealing with meetings and other issues. The team protocol is a living document. It should be revisited regularly and amended as necessary.

There is no doubt that people who are satisfied with their environment, and demonstrate it through team civility are more motivated and produce better results. As with other positive events, the benefits of civil behavior are synergistic and produce outcomes *vastly disproportionate* to the behavior itself.

Becoming a Team

"Speech! Speech!"

The thirty-five year veteran rose from his seat to address the crowd assembled for his retirement party. He'd risen from an entry-level position to executive management. He'd survived acquisitions, right sizing, reengineering and a host of other business phases long lost to memory. He'd seen it all, and in the end had triumphed. He made the usual speech—thanked everyone, praised the teamwork and fellowship. But he ended with a remarkable statement. He said, "I've been here thirty-five years and feel that I'm still learning the ropes. I hope it doesn't take me that long to learn how to retire!" He got a laugh, sat down, and the party continued. Largely missed by the revelers, however, was a profound insight about how teams become teams.

"Learning the ropes." Most people and organizations believe that learning the ropes is synonymous with orientation. It's the time-limited period in which someone new is introduced to the organization. This invariably includes satisfying the mechanical aspects of employment such as payroll and benefits, and usually includes a social aspect as well. The social component is typically less organized than the mechanical component and may range from coffee with co-workers to an after hours reception. The common factor is that orientation *happens* and then it's *over*. You've been oriented—so get to work! Sure, everyone recognizes that there will be a learning curve, but the expectation is that when your orientation is over you'll be a fully functioning team member.

And that is where our new retiree alerted us to something important. Learning the ropes, orientation, is a process that extends through the life of your assignment. It begins with a decision to hire you or assign you to a team, and continues until you leave the team or organization. It never ends. It can't.

Let's look first at how a new team orients. The team maker has work to be done. He determines the goal and identifies the initial skills necessary for accomplishment. He then assembles his core team. At this point team members are unknown to each other and are unfamiliar with the task. The team maker's responsibility is now twofold: *orient the members to each other and orient them to the task.*

Underlying this initial orientation is always the desire to *build confidence.* The members must learn enough about what each brings to the team to foster mutual respect, build rapport and facilitate delegation of responsibilities. The members must also clearly discern the goal and simultaneously begin developing the certainty that they can succeed. Many of these aspects can begin *before* the members first assemble. The more the team members know in advance, the more successful the orientation process. This is because advance information begins shaping member expectations immediately. By the time of the first meeting, positive expectations can be created and an initial level of confidence established. These individual expectations can then be used to jump-start the creation of the team's first common experiences. Members will come to the first meeting with *some* expectations, whether or not the team makers and leaders have provided advance information. In the absence of information, new members will typically have less confidence and commitment. They may also have an imprecise understanding of the goal and an initial reticence to participate fully. In effect, they'll want to test the waters before jumping in.

We'll discuss managing these first impressions at greater length later, but for now, team leaders should ensure that new members receive some form of advance information. Minimally it should include a clear statement of the team's goal. It should list the members, something about each one, and why each was selected for the team. It should briefly explain what is expected of the members and what the members can expect in return. Of course, the entire tone and presentation should be positive.

When the first impressions are well managed, it's easy to create the initial positive common experiences such as social events (celebration), training, or experiential learning opportunities. To the extent possible, these orienting efforts should help the team taste success. That's why associative experiences such as completion of a challenge course or an off site retreat work so well. They give the members opportunities to refine their working style in a risk free environment. Whatever the activity, the net result is always that the team knows another, knows what is expected, and comes away with a common experiential base as a team.

Now consider the orientation requirements when a new member joins an intact team. The situation may arise when a core member has been reassigned or when an associate will be joining the core for an extended period of time. In either case orientation must occur. On the most obvious level, the newcomer will be at an information disadvantage in terms of the task. The team veterans will have a deeper understanding of exactly where the project is and the nuances of how it got there. But more subtly, they'll know each other's responsibilities, strengths and weaknesses. They'll have common experiences that bind them in a unique team culture of their own making.

Because of this, the orientation must be painstakingly detailed. It must bring the new member up to date on the task and begin a process of reshaping the culture to include another point of view. This will begin by providing the new member with as much printed or on-line information as possible before the first meeting. At the first meeting the veterans should plan the equivalent of an *initiation*. This shouldn't be bizarre —no campfires and baying at the moon—but it should recognize that everything is changing. Remember WYSINWYG! The addition of a new team member will change things. On the basis of personality type alone, tremendous upheavals may be created. Imagine the impact of a firewall extravert joining a team of firewall introverts; or a strong intuitive joining a team of sensors. The comfortable relationships of the past will all have to be reworked in recognition of a new behavioral dynamic. The initiation is a means of creating a new set of common experiences—common to *all* the members of the team.

While thoughtful orientation to both the task and the team are important at the launch of a project, it doesn't end there. Throughout the life of the project an ongoing process of reorientation should occur. This reorientation serves a maintenance function. It keeps loose ends tied up and helps everyone stay sharp. The first aspect of continual reorientation is the regular *progress review*. It provides an opportunity to revisit the goal and make sure that everyone is still aligned toward successful completion. A second aspect is a *protocol* review.

The features that the team discusses for good citizenship should be reconsidered at intervals. Are the agreed upon elements working. Is there a problem that should be addressed or new elements added? Planning such reviews can often head off infighting or hurt feelings because members know with certainty that they'll have a chance to raise concerns.

Teams should also keep building their store of positive common experiences. These, of course, include regular celebrations, but might include ongoing training as well. This training might be directly related to the project or be designed to promote an imaginative stretch. In either case team culture is strengthened and confidence promoted.

The Citizenship Dividend

The journey up Mt. Fuji that started this work yielded a citizenship lesson as well. An odd thing happened when our little band of Fuji climbers returned to base. Because we'd had such an obviously good time, we became instant experts on climbing Mt. Fuji. Whether the issue was when to climb, what to wear, who to take along or how to get there, we were sought out for advice. Both friends and strangers saw us as people who had succeeded on the mountain and who could therefore be relied upon for sound information. We had become credible.

Credibility is an important, though perhaps unexpected, dividend of good team citizenship. A well structured and positively interacting team maximizes the chance for success by a creating a highly creditable unit. This is a self-reinforcing, cyclic process. When teams operate with high levels of good citizenship, members interact more frequently and share information more efficiently. These characteristics are applied to those outside the team as well. This openness and accuracy fosters trust. In an atmosphere of trust, teams set higher goals and consequently accomplish more. Greater achievement, in turn, spurs more cooperation and open communications. Credibility is very much a product of careful team assembly. Effective team makers won't ever leave this aspect to chance formation.

The Second Stop on the Assembly Line

Good citizenship is essential for effective teams. The environment in which members operate will tremendously shape the team's ability to succeed. Keep the following in mind when assembling the team:

1. Discuss and promote behaviors that show personal consideration
2. Discuss and promote professional standards of conduct
3. Begin orientation before members first meet
4. Create common experiences of success for the team
5. Ensure that everyone knows the goal and their responsibilities
6. Foster confidence and credibility by "reorienting" on a regular basis.

Work

We're right sized, have great attitudes and everyone is behaving well. Now what? What exactly do teams do? We can look back to our section on Chaos for an answer because the work of teams directly corresponds to the underlying structure of both organizations and personality. That is, *teams gather data and make decisions about planning, developing and operating projects or tasks.* The type of data and sophistication of the decision will largely determine how the team is assembled. Simply put, different types of *work* will require different types of *teams*.

As it relates to the business of team *work*, data-gathering and decision-making exist on a single continuum. At one end of this continuum is factual data-gathering and at the other end is subjective decision-making. Remember that this continuum represents *types* of work to be accomplished. The *type of work* will determine the *type of team* required to get the job done.

Let's illustrate this with the infamous, *"Great Chopstick Campaign."* A chopstick manufacturer wanted to boost sales through a new ad campaign. In order to help the advertising agency understand their product, the company planned to pull together all the details of the chopstick story and draft a powerful new slogan. The president was keen on teams and anxious to launch another one, but being a good planner, he first pondered his next move.

He decided that the most helpful information for the agency would be the product specifications. Just the facts. Perfect work for a cross-functional team! He reached for the phone, but hesitated. While a team could gather the data, he realized that he could just as easily get the information himself. Turning to his computer, he typed out an e-mail to his division chiefs asking that they reply back with their specification sheets. An hour later he scrolled through the specifications. He saw that his chopsticks were 12 inches long; cylindrical, tapered or, squared at one end and round at the other. He saw they were plastic, wood or lacquer; and either etched or color stamped. In short, not much on which to base an exciting ad campaign.

He wanted punch, flash and dazzle! He wanted creative, off the wall ideas! Assemble a team! He'd already selected seven names when he remembered something he'd learned long ago. Individuals working alone produce *two to four times* the number of ideas that people working in a group. On top of that, the quality of their ideas was consistently better. He turned again to his e-mail. His mailing list to company supervisors contained fifty names. He sent a message requesting each recipient take five minutes and describe every conceivable use of a chopstick they could think of. Anything goes.

Shortly he was inundated with ideas. Hundreds of them. Everything from shoveling rice and ladling soup, to using as tomato stakes, paint sticks, and kindling. Colorful ideas. Practical ideas. Creative ideas. But lots and lots and lots of them. More in fact than he could sort through. He recognized it in a flash. He needed—at last—a first tier, face-to-face core team.

Up to this point, he'd only needed his staff for *collaboration*. Everyone worked together, but independently, on a common goal. It was a matter of pulling information together rather than making decisions about it. Now what was called for was *coordination*. Ideas had to be cleaned up and organized. The president saw that he needed someone to determine and apply appropriate filters and criteria that would make the data valuable.

Even though decision-making was important at this point, the president knew it wouldn't require executive level insight. The task leant itself to straightforward, objective analysis. He by-passed his vice presidents and selected five junior employees—high-energy people who typically didn't have a chance to work on management project teams. He tasked them to consolidate redundancies, categorize what was left and then retain only the items that were possible, even though they might be improbable. (Chopsticks as a source for the mulch needed to organically garden on Mars wouldn't make *this* cut.)

The eager team leader distributed the massive lists and project assignment to the other members. She tasked everyone to complete the assignment individually and to send the results back to her for consolidation. When she received the material back, the leader saw much commonality. It was an easy task to consolidate the data; highlighting both areas of convergence and divergence. She sent the consolidated material back to everyone for review before their first face-to-face meeting. During the meeting, the team made quick work of refining the filters, categorizing and identifying all the possible uses of chopsticks.

The president was delighted with the results. The final categories were food consumption implements, gardening aids and incendiary devices. Each category contained many possible, though often improbable, uses for their chopsticks. The data was now manageable, but what was to be done with it? How would it shape the campaign? Did it reflect the true nature of the company? Could everyone get behind it?

The president decided to float a trial balloon by distributing the report to the vice presidents. The response was immediate and forceful. Everyone, it seemed, had a strong opinion. Time for another team. This time the president relied on his management team. As an intact team, they were comfortable working together and had forged a healthy, positive culture. The goal now was to decide how to frame the data for use in the ad campaign. There was no right answer only a *preferred* one.

To identify the preference would require careful discernment of the market, company culture, and agreement about which approach would generate the most interest. Importantly, a decision would require *persuasion* as a prerequisite to consensus. Whatever the outcome, everyone would have to be convinced it was the best approach in order to ensure buy-in. The president knew that in order to achieve these aims, a face-to-face meeting was essential. Only that forum provided the social cues such as tone, gesture and expression that prove so powerful in communicating one's point of view. While these cues can dampen creativity, they are indispensable when expressing convictions.

The president held his meeting. Everyone was thoroughly familiar with the issues before arriving and a spirited discussion was the order of the day. In the end the team decided that, "Chopsticks—the tool that helps you grow, cook, and eat your food," was the slogan that would send just the right message. And it did.

We've been discussing how team structure should reflect the type of work the team is trying to accomplish. When data is factual and easy to access, small, second tier teams can do the job. As more data and more abstract data are required, larger second tier teams produce the best results. Moving from simply acquiring information to making basic decisions about it generates a need for first tier teams. When there is a right answer to be found, coordination is the key to putting the necessary pieces of the puzzle together. On simple problems, second tier teams are still effective, but with an increase in complexity, the first tier (or an organizational hybrid) becomes more important. Finally, first tier teams, meeting face-to-face, make the best decisions when subjective judgments and persuasive argument are required.

The organizational subtext is that *teams should never meet face-to-face unless absolutely necessary*. The numbers are worth repeating: face-to-face teams produce two to four times less, and what they produce is of poorer quality than individuals working alone and then pooling their resources. First tier teams should never be used for creative idea generation or simple problem solving. *Meetings are best suited for subjective decision-making.*

Evaluation

There is a final aspect of teamwork that should be considered. That aspect is evaluation. At the most basic level, teamwork is evaluated on the basis of *speed, quantity and quality.* That is, how fast is the task done, how much is accomplished, how good are the results? Ford's assembly line dealt with all three. How fast? One every 24 seconds. How many? Fifteen million. How good? You can still find them on the road today.

When it comes to teamwork, the measures may be applied separately or all together. If the president of the chopstick company had wanted ideas quickly, without regard to quantity or quality, he could have stepped outside his office and polled everyone within sight. His decision to use an e-mail list compromised speed for quantity; (although it was still faster than calling a meeting). His decision to filter the list compromised both speed and quantity in favor of a quality product that would be more immediately applicable to the goal. Circumstance will dictate which measure is most critical at any given time and what the appropriate *balance* between them will be.

A study of the relationship between quantity and quality, however, has revealed an interesting phenomenon. Quantity measures the team's output. It may be units, dollars, items, or even a single report. It is the tangible product of the completed assignment. Quality measures the error rate of the output. All things being equal, teams seek to simultaneously maximize quantity and quality. Sadly, all things are almost never equal, and *with complex, time sensitive and difficult tasks, teams will invariably sacrifice quality for quantity.*

The studies showed that when faced with difficult quality *and* quantity goals, quantity performance increased, but quality performance did not.

When quantity goals were easy and quality goals difficult, quality performance increased. Interestingly, when both goals were easy, quality also under-performed quantity. Apparently, teams are unable to optimize performance in both areas simultaneously.

Also noteworthy was the fact that *as quantity goals became more difficult, teams begin to restrict their data-gathering activities.* With the addition of time constraints, they became increasingly concerned with *demonstrating immediate progress.* This progress was usually at the expense of any data-gathering that might make task completion easier. This urgency even drove out minimal planning efforts and thus decreased the likelihood of success, to say the least of producing a quality product.

This phenomenon is regularly demonstrated during experiential learning exercises. When the team is tasked with getting all members over a difficult obstacle in a short period of time, they invariable rush into the task before thinking it through. In the absence of a plan, they miscue one another, make multiple errors and rarely complete the assignment. Even when prompted to spend time in preplanning they seem compelled to show progress instead.

Implications for team assembly are clear. Team makers must be clear about how the project is to be measured. Certainly, when speed and quantity are the primary measures, second tier teams will be preferable. If quality is to be a factor at all, specific quality goals will have to be formulated and communicated to the team. In the absence of such guidance it's a virtual certainty that quality with be limited.

The Third Stop on the Assembly Line

The great chopstick campaign provides some salient points for station team assembly:

1. Match the team structure to the work needed to be done
2. Use second tier teams when *collaboration* is required
   - Small teams when data is easily accessible
   - Large teams when creative or high quantity is desired

3. Projects that require *coordination* to identify a correct answer can use first tier, second tier or hybrid structures depending on complexity

4. Always use first tier teams when *subjective decisions* must be reached and when *persuasion* is an element

5. Never hold a meeting unless absolutely necessary.

6. Understand and balance the requirement for speed, quantity and quality

7. If quality is desired set explicit quality goals.

The stops on this assembly line provide the mechanics of setting up high functioning station teams. Team makers and leaders must consider team size, citizenship and the type of work to be accomplished as a prerequisite to putting people together to accomplish a goal. Careful team assembly will produce results as remarkable today as the Model T was in the Teens!

MOTIVATION AT THE FIFTH STATION

He was a beekeeper with a flair for adventure. As a boy he dreamed of courageous exploits and took the daring British explorer, Sir Ernest Henry Shackleton as a role model. As a man, he redefined post war heroism by his climb to the top of the world. His name was Edmund Hillary, and on the eve of the coronation of Queen Elizabeth II, he became the first man to scale Mt. Everest.

Mountain climbing was something Hillary came upon by chance. A high school outing when he was sixteen brought him his first exposure to mountains, ice and snow. It was his first real adventure and it produced a passion for mountaineering that would steadily grow. He began climbing in New Zealand, moved on to the Alps and finally challenged the Himalayas. By the time of his assault on Everest, he had climbed 11 mountains with heights in excess of 20,000 feet.

But Mt. Everest was something all together different. At 29,028 feet above sea level, its summit was believed to be the highest point on earth. No man had ever climbed that high before and there was serious speculation by physiologists that life couldn't be sustained at the summit—with or without supplemental oxygen. The fact that no one had yet made it to the top was not simply because no one had tried. Between 1920 and 1952 seven expeditions had made the attempt. None had succeeded. In 1924, the effort cost famous climber, George Leigh-Mallory, his life. The 1952 Swiss expedition was forced back a thousand feet short of the mark.

Hillary participated in Everest reconnaissance expeditions in both 1951 and 1952. As a result, he was invited to join a 1953 expedition sponsored by the Joint Himalayan Committee of the Alpine Club of Great Britain and the Royal Geographic Society. Though the team was highly skilled and well equipped, by May 29, only Hillary and Nepalese Sherpa, Tenzing Norgay continued toward the peak. At 11:30 that morning, they reached the summit. Hillary later recalled that he felt a sense of satisfaction and a little surprise standing there at the top of the world. After Norgay buried some chocolate and other sweets, the two began their equally challenging descent. It wasn't until they reached base camp and heard of their success on the BBC that they felt the full, exhilarating impact of their accomplishment.

The victory over Everest changed everything. Hillary was lifted from obscurity to international fame and knighthood. He went on, like his hero Shackleton, to explore the Antarctic, and actually led the first mechanized expedition to the South Pole. There were, of course, other mountains to climb, and Hillary did so. Yet the accolades and opportunities for new adventures don't begin to explain why Hillary climbed the mountain. Even hindsight doesn't provide an answer.

Why *did* Hillary climb? Why do hundreds of others try every year? Why, at tremendous expense, would anyone place his or her life in such a precarious balance? Why Everest? What's the gain? Where's the payoff? What's the *motivation*?

It's All About Motivation

The question really *is* about motivation. After all, what impels someone to climb a mountain, or go to college, or save for a car, or learn a new language or anything of a thousand things? What is it that moves someone to action from a position of comfortable stasis? The answer is *motivation*. Motivation is the process of stimulating you to action. It takes a need, desire or some other impulse and incites a response. Motivation is the high-octane fuel of success and, as such, it's vital that individuals and teams capitalize on its power.

Often motivation seems to occur spontaneously—the result of apparently random events. But random motivation isn't the stuff of greatness—to say the least of profitability, innovation and success. It's imperative that team makers and leaders cultivate and nurture motivation throughout the life of a project. Fortunately, motivation is relatively easy to create. In fact, it can be described in a formula: $M = (D+A)U$. That is, *motivation* equals *dissonance* plus *accountability*, multiplied by *urgency*. This is the DNA of motivation. It's the essence of what will fire individual imagination and resiliently drive action. Contained within this simple formula are the seeds of phenomenal success.

Dissonance

Dissonance is the first piece of the formula and one of the most powerful single influences experienced by all humankind. It is the means of finding the prerequisite *motive* needed to motivate. Musically, dissonance is a combination of tones, suggesting unrelieved tension that cries out for resolution. Audiences often find it more annoying than entertaining. They want it to end. Generally speaking, this is the effect of dissonance under any circumstances. Dissonance is an itch that demands to be scratched; a rising pressure that must be vented; a soldier out of step in the parade who must skip-step back into ranks. Dissonance creates a discordant state in which there is an absence of harmony, agreement, or, consistency.

Such a condition creates an *imbalance*. When we discussed balance as a *Fifth Station* principle, we noted that the yearning for balance grips people at the most elemental levels. The desire for balance shapes our behavior biologically, intellectually and spiritually. Thus, dissonance triggers an innate response. It arouses us and drives us to close the gap, or in other words, to satisfy our desire.

It was the imbalance between extreme asceticism and indolence that led Prince Siddartha to find enlightenment through the *middle way*. In fact, the *Four Noble Truths* of Buddhism have at their core, the concept of dissonance. The Truths are: 1) suffering is universal, 2) the cause of suffering is craving, 3) the cure for suffering is the elimination of craving, 4) the way to achieve the elimination of craving is to follow the Middle Way.

As a description of dissonance, we might reinterpret the Truths as follows; 1) dissonance is a universal human experience, 2) the cause of dissonance is desire, 3) the cure for desire is satisfaction, 4) the way to achieve satisfaction is by pursuing a balanced goal. At its most basic level, then, dissonance is the gap between what *is* and what's *desired*. Dissonance is the recognition that the current condition is not the desired condition. Things aren't what they could be. This recognition of imbalance fires our innate tendency to restore equilibrium.

Obviously, the object of our desire must be something worthwhile. There will be no motivation to restore balance if the *as is* and *desired* states are seen as roughly comparable. If they're comparable, there isn't any real imbalance. Similarly, if the "desired" state is inferior to the status quo, there won't be any motivation to move in that direction. Almost no one leaves the recliner to clean the garage during the Super Bowl (no matter how boring the game is!).

The greater the desire, the stronger the drive for satisfaction. The greater the dissonance, the greater the motivation to succeed. This is the force that pushed Hillary up Everest. The strength to cover the last leg was the product of a very clear objective and the equally clear realization that no one had ever succeeded and that there was no higher mountain to climb. Those elements created a *gap* far wider than any ice crevasse ever faced by Hillary and Norgay.

Dissonance is an easy condition to create. Advertisers do it all the time through their, "bigger, better, brighter, and newer" campaigns. The idea is to make people dissatisfied with a current commodity or situation in order to get them to purchase a different one. Ronald Reagan capitalized on the strategy during his first election campaign. When he asked the American people, "are you better off today than you were four years ago," he opened an enormous dissonance gap. Carter himself identified it as a national, "malaise," so it was hardly surprising when people decided that their *as is* was something less than *desired*. The result was eight years for Ron and early retirement for Jimmy. Business does the same thing through bonus systems, incentive plans and promotion tracks. Multi-level marketers, in particular, have honed the idea into high art. The entire pitch is aimed at convincing people that that they could be *much* better off than they actually are, if only they would cultivate their, "down-lines."

Accountability

Dissonance alone can motivate, but coupled with *accountability* it becomes an almost irresistible source of motivation. Basically, *accountability* means you are answerable or responsible for what happens. Accountability links the individual and the outcome. The closer the link, the greater the accountability. Thus, it's not surprising that individual accountability is stronger than team accountability. Dissonance arouses the *awareness* of an imbalance, while accountability *personalizes* it.

The primary benefit of accountability is that it fosters *complex thinking*. This begins to happen when you anticipate having to explain your actions. Almost everyone has had this experience. Imagine that your boss has just called and asked you to attend a department head meeting during which company-wide budget overruns will be discussed. How will you prepare? You might quickly review your own budget if you have time, but chances are that you'll simply show up to hear what will be said. Even though you know you have budgetary responsibility, "company-wide," problems pack pretty general levels of accountability. Consequently, you probably won't think too much about the meeting in advance and are likely to do little more than just respond to what is discussed.

Now imagine that your boss has called and asked to see you to discuss the budget overruns in *your* department. Without doubt, the adrenaline will kick in and you'll do all sorts of preparation. You'll gather your facts.

You'll try to anticipate questions and possible criticisms. You'll mentally rehearse your explanations of what you did and why. You might even try to poke holes in your own arguments to spot weaknesses or inconsistencies. This is what complex thinking means and it's definitely a result of accountability.

When held accountable for their actions, individuals and teams tend to do the following:

1. They carefully define the problem or situation. They gather facts. They pay attention to context and history. They stay close to the realities of the issue.

2. They become sensitive to possibilities as well as actualities. They dampen their own biases by giving an objective hearing to all reasonable alternatives. Even when they have a preference, they are careful to assess it against competing ideas.

3. They analyze closely and look for inconsistencies. They weigh the pros and cons of each case. They look for what's reasonable and consider the costs of not acting.

4. They consider the alternatives against the backdrop of the organization's culture, values and beliefs. They look for subjective consistency and the broader impact of their choices. They assess commitment and support.

The benefits of complex thinking are enormous. It's the best way to consistently make the right decisions and to build consensus. When we've used dissonance to clarify motive; and accountability to personalize it, we are likely to find success within our grasp.

Accountability misapplied, however, poses its own set of problems. The difficulty arises when accountability becomes *punitive*. This happens when fear is introduced to the equation. The fear can be of anything: job loss, demotion, the boss' wrath or humiliation. The result is always the same. When the price of failure is punishment, the benefits of accountability mutate. Where once it powerfully motivated change, now it becomes a seedbed for caution and adherence to the status quo. Individuals and teams that are fearful, usually gather far more information than is necessary. This often leads to over-interpretation or the loss of important data in a sea of unimportant information.

Under the pressure of extreme accountability, confidence flags and second-guessing becomes common. Isolation sets in, a "bunker mentality," develops and enemies are found everywhere. Data is easily misread and far more negative possibilities are found than actually exit. Grandiose thinking is not unusual and deep meaning is discovered in data where none exists. There is obsession over minor details while significant data is ignored.

Fear-based accountability can also foster a reluctance to make any decision at all. Individuals and teams may resist making a decision that could subject them to criticism. At best, they adopt a middle of the road position (not to be confused with a *balanced* position) that is designed to please everyone rather than one that might offend someone. The bottom line is that fear leads to impaired decision-making and a resistance to change.

There is a final pitfall associated with accountability that team makers and team leaders should keep in mind. When things are going wrong, teams tend to share the blame for problems and by doing so, dissipate the sense of accountability that might have led to a solution. Simply put, *the farther accountability is removed from the individual, the less likely it is to foster complex thinking*. In the face of difficulties, individuals that feel responsible are likely to persevere toward finding a solution—think of Hillary and Norgay on the final ascent. Groups and teams, however, tend to generalize culpability. The effect is to diminish accountability. In essence, everyone is held accountable with the net effect being that no one is accountable. In this way, accountability is rationalized away as unimportant and dissonance is correspondingly weakened.

Problems aside, accountability is a team maker and team leader's indispensable tool for fostering the kind of complex thinking necessary for closing the dissonance gap. Accountability is a dynamic motivating force. Pitfalls can easily be avoided by ensuring that accountability is never fear based and by making team members individually as well as corporately responsible for the quality of their performance.

Urgency

Urgency is the third element in our equation. As we've seen, identifying the motive for our actions, the desired state, provides a degree of motivation in and of itself. Establishing accountability further incites motivation by fostering complex thinking about that desired state. Yet we're also aware that many people who know where they want to be and know that they are responsible for getting there, never quite make it because they just don't get around to doing it. What they lack is a *sense of urgency* about arriving at the desired end state.

The word urgent comes to us from Latin where it meant *to push*. That's what urgency does to dissonance and accountability; it pushes them to deliver results. It multiplies their power by adding parameters of *importance* and *immediacy*. Latin roots are again helpful. The root of importance meant *to carry in*. Today we use the word to identify something that carries great weight or significance. The Latin root of immediacy meant, *not in the middle*. In other words, something that has arrived—something here right now. Today the word means essentially the same thing. It carries an imperative sense. It refers to something that must be attended to at once, or without delay.

Think of an old Roman carrying something into his house. Urgency comes along and pushes him inside. Now the Roman comes home from a business trip. He stands on the threshold and urgency shoves him through the doorway. Awfully rude in both cases, but that's what urgency does. It makes the important more important, and the immediate, more immediate. Urgency always raises the stakes a little higher.

Sadly, urgency is often mistaken and its vitality wasted on things that are *neither* important nor immediate. The single greatest villain in this regard is the telephone. Let's face it, a ringing telephone seems urgent. People routinely fly, dripping wet from showers, miss critical punch lines from their favorite sitcoms, and tear themselves away from the most tender of embraces to answer that ringing phone. So many dinners sat cooling while calls from tele-marketers were answered that legislation was required to limit their access. Just think of how much energy is wasted retrieving meaningless phone calls, and yet the race to the phone goes on. That's the bad news. The good news is that our zeal for answering the phone underscores the power urgency has to motivate worthwhile behavior.

The problem with the phone is that we can't really ascertain the importance of the call until we pick it up. After all, that "unavailable" on your caller-ID might be someone selling can openers or it could be Ed McMahon calling to give you a million dollars. The ring provides all the immediacy we need because it won't ring forever (it only seems that way) and once it stops, we've missed our window of opportunity. So, unless you're expecting a call or are on call, we could say that a ringing phone is something that is immediate but not important. Thus, even though some folks seem genetically hard-wired to answer the phone, it's not really urgent that they do so. Responding with urgency to the immediate but unimportant only wastes resources and is ultimately de-motivating.

Sometimes, things can be important but not immediate. Let's take an example from the healthcare industry. The Joint Commission on Accreditation of Healthcare Organizations accredits virtually all public and private hospitals. Accreditation surveys occur every three years. In order to remain financially viable, hospitals must remain accredited. In this regard, the successful completion of the survey is an important objective from the moment the last one is completed. But three years flunks the immediacy test. Everyone knows that passing the next survey is the desired state, and those responsible know who they are, but preparations are in the realm of the routine. The survey is important, but not immediate. It therefore lacks a motivating sense of urgency. Of course, as the survey date approaches, the immediacy will increase until a clear sense of urgency develops. At that point, the benefits of having a clearly defined goal and specific accountability will produce dynamic results. At this stage, however, there is little urgency to spend time on survey preparations at the expense of other, more immediate tasks.

Let's consider Hillary and Norgay back on Mt. Everest. They sit at High Camp waiting for a break in the weather. The climbing season, at best, is only a few weeks long. To make it the weather has to be just right. And so they wait. Are they motivated? Let's check the equation. First the *motive*—to reach the summit and safety return. Definitely clear. *Accountability*: they, and no one else, will determine if and when to climb. As they wait, both mentally calculate and recalculate their options. Sense of *urgency*: overwhelming!

This is the most critical and important leg of the climb. If this doesn't happen the expedition has failed. Though unique in its own right, climbing part way up Mt. Everest doesn't have quite the cachet of being the first to make it to the top. In terms of immediacy, this is about as immediate as it gets. The time is now. It's important, and it's immediate, and the mix creates a combustible sense of urgency.

Too often team makers and team leaders leave urgency to chance. They just assume teams will understand the priorities. They forget that we live in a WYSINWYG world. Every day, in every land, workers overlook things that seem self-evident to the boss. The best corrective is to clarify the twin elements of importance and immediacy. Teams that clearly understand the relative importance of each of their assignments and who have no doubts about deadlines and due dates, will generate the right level of urgency for every project. The key is to give them all the pertinent details. Generalities around issues of importance and immediacy only produce disappointment. Careful attention to the dynamics of urgency will, on the other hand, produce turbo charged motivation.

That's the motivation equation. Begin by using *dissonance* to determine motive. That is, to identify the *as is* and the *desired*, end state. Secondly, promote complex thinking about the motive by assigning specific *accountability*. Finally, give the whole thing a push by creating a sense of *urgency* based on the importance of the task and the immediacy of the required action.

Light Bulbs, Lasers and Goals

Hillary and Norgay faced extraordinary physical and psychological challenges during their climb, but their motivation was clear. They always knew where they where, and where they wanted to be (alternately the summit or the base!). Bringing this degree of clarity to a project is one of the fundamental challenges of team makers and leaders. The most successful teams will always operate with a lively, yet *focused* motivation. In some ways, motivation is like turning on a light bulb. Light from the bulb instantly floods the room. The same light, however, when *focused*, becomes a laser with vastly more powerful applications. The ability to create this laser-like focus determines who will reach the summit and who will simply mark time in the base camp.

The single best way to achieve focus is to set realistic *goals*. The word, "goal," is one of the oldest in the English language. Originally it meant, "barrier," or, "boundary." Today we think of a goal as an objective or purpose to which we direct our energy. The older version, however, imparts a fuller flavor to the concept of *Fifth Station* goals. At the *Fifth Station*, goals always follow motivation. That is, they are always set at the far boundaries of our capabilities because they reflect not only where we *are*, but also where we *want* to be.

To illustrate, let's use a British example. When the Emperor Hadrian visited Britain in the year 122 C.E., the region marked the far northern boundary of the Roman Empire. Hadrian ordered that a fortified wall be built marking that boundary. Over the next six years, Roman legionnaires constructed a 73-mile wall that ran from Wallsend-on-Tyne in the east to Bowness-on-Solway in the west. This fifteen foot high stone wall at the edge of the empire became known as, "Hadrian's Wall."

Hadrian's Wall stood at the extreme frontier of the empire. It was geographically at the far end of Roman supply lines, authority and culture. Its distance from Rome symbolically indicated the vastness and power of the empire. It communicated the empire's expansive *stretch* throughout the known world. Because the frontier was so far from Rome, it physically and psychologically energized the population tasked with its maintenance. Once the boundary was set, it became a clear marker for future conquest.

Fifth Station goals do much the same thing. They clearly mark the *frontiers* of our thinking, capability and vision. *Fifth Station* goals bring our challenges into focus. They push beyond the status quo and define our attainable stretch. They provide a springboard for our planning and the clarity needed to transform undifferentiated motivation into success.

Precision is the driving force in goal setting. Simply put, the more precise your goal, the more likely you are to succeed. Thus, effective goals have only two requirements; they should be as *specific as possible and objectively measurable*.

Determining a goal's specificity isn't always as easy as it sounds. Goal specificity can be measured on a continuum that ranges from *performance* to *learning*. Performance goals require action. They call upon you to demonstrate, prove or validate a particular course of action or ability. Typically, performance is measured in terms of *speed, quantity and quality*.

If, for example, the task is to generate new product ideas, your team might opt for *speed*: brainstorm for five minutes. They might opt for *quantity*: each member will produce ten suggestions at the next meeting. Or, the team might opt for *quality*: each member will submit one feasible proposal. The team could even opt for all three: we'll produce three feasible alternatives in thirty minutes. Performance goals are almost always *objective*. Implicit in the performance goal is a pass/fail standard, or a single right answer. You either make it or you don't. Not surprisingly, when the standard is this clear and people believe that it's doable, they will exert tremendous effort to succeed.

The other end of the continuum marks goals that are *learning* oriented. They require you to develop an awareness, appreciation or understanding of something. The primary aim here is not action, but learning or mastery. The skills required involve *judgment, analysis,* and *creativity.* The goal tends to require a good deal of *subjectivity.* For example a corporate team might be tasked to develop a vision statement. The task will involve identifying the company culture, the culture of the market place, and making futuristic projections about both. Now there is no clear pass/fail standard or apparent right answer. The standard seems to be, "do the best you can."

Yet even with learning goals, precision is an ally. In our WYSINWYG world, even the most general tasking carries with it some standard—even if the standard is unstated. Assume that you are working on deadline to compile a major report. It's Monday and your boss approaches and says, "I know you're busy right now, but I'd like you to get a feel for the problems we're having with the new product roll out and let me know what you think. No hurry; do it when you can." On Friday, the boss calls for your research and seems surprised that you haven't even started it yet. Turns out he needs it Monday morning, and that "get a feel for" was really supposed to be a detailed analysis (with Power Point slides!).

The challenge is to make every goal as specific as possible without narrowing it to the point of irrelevance. Is the goal "awareness," or developing a course of action? Does, "understanding," mean exposure to a product, or mastering its technical vocabulary? To some extent, getting specific means making every goal a performance goal. It means searching out the *action* in every motivational impulse. Whenever general words creep into a goal statement, they should be challenged and narrowed to the most specific level possible. This is the best way of ensuring success, because it's the only way of making the outcome transparent to all players.

Once you've determined what exactly you're trying to do, it's time to determine how you'll know when you've done it. To this end, every goal should include an *objective measure of success*. We've already noted that action oriented performance goals are measured in terms of speed, quantity and quality. The same measures apply when outcomes are apparently subjective. For example, if your program goal is to improve employee morale, you might measure results through pre and post program surveys. If the Vicar's goal is to instill a deeper appreciation for stewardship, success might be measured through increased offerings or hours volunteered following his sermon. Again, the challenge is to be as specific in the measure as you are in the outcome.

Probably the most significant aspect of any measure is the stretch that it includes. Remember that *goals follow motivation*. In order to be effective, there must be a clear distinction between the *as is* and the *desired*. Motivation is strongest when achieving the desired involves an *attainable stretch*. If the desired seems beyond grasp, the effect is demotivating. Virtually every athletic team, whether pro or amateur, has difficulty playing if they believe their defeat is inevitable. They'll go through the motions, but without heart. Conversely if the goal is within easy grasp, *urgency* is dampened and there is little motivation to perform. Again, virtually no sports team is immune from defeat when they assume an easy win. More than once a feisty opponent has trounced a complacent champion. Only when the athletes believe that they can prevail through diligent application of their skills is victory clearly on the radar. Picture any contender in any Olympic sport.

One benefit of including objective measurements in your goal is that people are aware of their level of performance. Dissonance is an evaluative standard. It's present when people assess their current state against the desired state. For this reason, people must be aware of their distance from the goal in order to be motivated by it. As movement toward the goal proceeds, evaluation will be an ongoing aspect of motivation. This is much like setting a goal to run a mile. If, as you run, you have no idea of the distance covered or the time elapsed, it will be hard to be motivated by the goal. For all you know, when you stop running you may have run a half-mile or two miles. In any event, the goal ceases to have meaning. The goal motivates only to the extent that you are challenged by what you *are* doing as opposed to what you'd *like* to be doing. Knowing that you are succeeding heightens motivation by fostering confidence. High confidence results in a willingness to assume greater challenges and more difficult goals.

As with most things, goals can be made very complicated. At the *Fifth Station* there just isn't any reason to make it harder than it has to be. First, make sure your goal *follows* the motivational impulse. That is, there should be a sharp distinction between the *as is* and the *desired* at the source. There should be an established *accountability* and a *sense of urgency* before even bothering to frame the goal. With those prerequisites, make your goal as *specific* as possible by clearly describing the desired outcome. Match the outcome with an objective *measure* of success that provides an *attainable stretch* from the current *as is*. The result will be laser-like alignment and a very high probability of success.

Before moving on, it's worth reflecting the critical importance of goals. We can find an easy illustration in our current political scene. Earlier we noted how Ronald Reagan created motivation for change by contrasting the "as is" under Jimmy Carter with what most Americans "desired." The fact that Reagan was able to galvanize the American public is testament to the lively political discussion that is an omnipresent feature of our culture. Every day literally tens of millions of people tune into radio talk shows to vicariously participate in the debate. Thousands of those actually get on air to state their case. Pathetically few, however, actually vote. Most believe their vote doesn't count—that they can't really influence anything. They couldn't be more wrong. In cities across the country, including America's major population centers, just a hand full of votes are deciding critical local races. At both the local and state level, special interest groups who recognize that it only requires getting a few votes to swing an election are dominating elected bodies such as school boards. Of course, the 2000 Presidential race proved that individual votes matter even in national elections.

Let's evaluate the motivational differences between the average voter and the special interest voter. The average voter has an opinion about how things are—he's for or against it. Thus, he'll either vote to keep things the same or to change them. The special interest voter feels the same way, however she has a goal. She's interested in a specific candidate in a specific race. Because of this focus, she'll engage in a wide variety of activities designed to help her candidate win. The candidate who relies on local endorsements and Election Day placards doesn't have a chance against someone with goal-focused supporters. It's the believers who'll go out and get commitment from the uncommitted and more importantly, bring in the voters who would not otherwise have voted. The lesson is this, whether in politics or anything else, those without goals will always be subject to those with goals.

Did You Say 300%?

To this point we've looked at the DNA of motivation and seen how goals can provide laser-like focus, but what about implementation? How do we actually go about achieving our goals? The answer is through planning. This should come as no surprise, as every goal contains a nascent plan. Since goals tell us where we are going and provide an objective measure of success, they suggest the strategy that we'll need to follow. With very simple goals, plan and goal are synonymous. However, as the complexity of the goal increases, the requirement for a separate plan grows as well. Let's illustrate the progression with an ambitious fun runner.

Assume you're a casual runner. Over the years you've developed a comfortable routine. Your typical run is three miles, on the high school track, in twenty-four minutes. Despite your relative youth, you have become increasingly concerned about the geriatric set routinely lapping you. As you approach the track, you realize tonight will be different! Your goal is three miles in twenty-three minutes!

Let's see how this goal stacks up with what we already know. First, it *follows* motivation. It was your competitive nature that fostered the disharmony associate with being *passed* by more people than *you* passed. The dissonance led to the goal. The goal also establishes clear *accountability*. Your feet are on the line. No one can do this but you. It will be your success or failure—and yours alone. The *feedback* will be immediate. The stopwatch doesn't lie. Finally, the goal establishes a sense of *urgency*. It will happen in the next twenty-seven minutes if for no other reason than you're already standing on the starting line. Our DNA motivational stew is definitely brewing. Secondly, the goal itself; it certainly is specific: three miles, on the high school track, in twenty-three minutes. It is also *objectively measurable*. At the end of the run you will know with high accuracy if you were successful or not. Importantly, the measure also includes the *stretch*. The goal pushes your personal frontiers, but is *attainable*

This very simple, but specific goal accomplishes everything anyone could hope for. It identifies the desired state, levels accountability, fosters a sense of urgency and is clearly focused. (Although cutting a full minute off your time is easier said than done.) It's also interesting, however, in what it doesn't require. It doesn't require a plan. No real strategy is needed. The goal requires only simple performance. With effort and persistence success is likely. If more is required, it's simply a matter of working harder. Goal and plan are one.

Preplanning

There comes a point, however, when working harder isn't as helpful as working smarter. As the goal becomes more complex, the question, "how am I going to do this," must be answered before acting. Such goals usually include several alternatives, although the strengths and weaknesses of each are quickly apparent. There is also a comfortable margin for error. If the alternative doesn't work out, another can be easily substituted. What is needed is a basic plan.

Flush with the success of completing your run in twenty-three minutes, you establish a new goal: to run a 5K race in a month. To begin with, let's look at what remains the same. The initial motivation is created by the desire to run faster. Accountability remains the same and the feedback will be immediate. The goal brings the motivation into focus. The goal is *performance* oriented—it requires you act. It's *objective, measurable* and contains *stretch*. The *first* major difference is in the sense of *urgency*. With a one-month time horizon the urgency dissipates. It will grow stronger as the race approaches, but here is not the immediacy of the first goal in which performance was imminent. The *second* major difference is that the new goal requires the implementation of a *plan*.

Running a 5K is a bit more complicated than your routine run. For one thing, the course will be more challenging than the track. It may be pavement and include hills. It may have 90-degree turns that will slow the pack. There may be potholes or speed bumps ready to twist the unwary ankle. The volume of runners will present another problem. Your solitary laps on the track offer tremendous opportunities to control your pace. A crowded 5K on the other hand, presents innumerable opportunities to slow you down. Now pulling a full minute off your regular time will require *more than effort*; it will require a *plan*. You'll have to study the course and locate the points where geography will work against you. You'll have to find the choke points where the pack is likely to slow down. Most importantly, you'll have to figure out a way around all the walkers who insist on lining up in front! Success will demand that you have a strategy and that you implement it. A collateral benefit of your plan is that it fosters a sense of urgency by alerting you to the complexities of the goal. In this case, you might discover that the challenges of the race itself will require you to train for a twenty-two minute 5K in order to actually do it in twenty-three minutes on race day. Because of the one-month time horizon, your sense of urgency was dissipated, but the plan provides a corrective.

With goals of *moderate complexity*, such as this one, most of the planning can be done in advance. This is called *pre-planning*. It can happen when most of the goal's variables are known beforehand. In this case, you'll know the day, time, route, and approximate race size with a high degree of certainty. You'll also be able to assess likely weather conditions and your training readiness. With this information you'll be able to confidently plan your race day strategy. By the time you show up, you'll only have to perform. Your pre-planning will, in effect, reduce a moderately complex goal to a simple one at the point of implementation.

Concurrent Planning

The race went well. You feel like a champion. Now you decide that in twelve months you'll run your first marathon. Not only will you run, but also you'll finish in four hours. Again, this goal has much in common with the others; it follows *motivation*, establishes *accountability* and provides for *feedback*. It's also *performance* related, objectively *measurable* and includes *stretch*. Importantly, with a time horizon of a year, there is little immediate urgency. However, due to the *complexity* of the goal, without some sense of urgency the likelihood of success is *nil*.

The delay of only a few months could doom the entire enterprise. Thus, it's *imperative* to have a plan. But this goal is complicated. The time span, training requirements and the marathon itself, make it impossible to simply implement a strategy. What is required *is a strategy about the goal itself*. That is, it's more important initially, to plan how to run *a* marathon than *the* marathon. The question now becomes, not, "*how* are we going to do it," but "*what* exactly are we trying to do?"

Answering this question will require more *theoretical* than practical skill. *Judgment* becomes important as right and wrong answers are hard to find. The search for strategies about the goal will be more *subjective* and *intuitive.* With high complexity goals, some degree of specificity will have to be sacrificed. This is particularly true in situations where there are many possible alternatives, the best one is not apparent, and the chance for retrying alternatives is limited. In such cases, specific goals might actually limit the search for the best alternative and create a sense of urgency that pushes the team before they have all the data.

A different kind of planning is required for highly complex goals. Because so many variable remain unknown, preplanning will be less effective. What is required is a highly flexible, simple preplan that relies on *concurrent planning* for detail. Concurrent planning is simply a planning process that accompanies actual implementation. In other words, *you plan as you go along.* As new data becomes available, you amend your original plan to fit the new data. For example, you may have initially planned to work up to a six-mile run after three months of training. You discover, instead, that because of your fitness level, you're running six miles after only eight weeks of training. Rather than stick to your old training schedule, your amend it to reflect your new capabilities.

Concurrent planning always works best with a series of *interim goals.* Interim goals are prearranged review points where progress is measured against the original goal and goal revisions are made. Remember the more specific the goal, the better. With highly complex goals we start general and run the attendant risk of staying that way. Concurrent planning is the means of applying new data to increase specificity. Interim goals are the means of making this happen.

Another benefit of interim goals is that they provide a chance to make "go—no go," decisions. Sometimes, despite our best intentions, a project just isn't going to work. The goal may prove to be impossible, irrelevant or imprudent. Rather than continuing onward, a decision might have to be made to stop the project. This isn't always easy. Projects have a tendency to take on lives of their own. Unless interim review points are established as a part of pre-planning and unless they include specific achievement goals, unproductive projects may continue long after they should have simply disappeared. If after seven months of training, you still can't break the three-mile barrier, it might be time to abandon the marathon dream and work on something else.

The plan about running *a* marathon will address all the complexities. Training schedules, milestones, weight, diet, shoes, and general race strategies will all be considered. Interim goals will be established and a reasonable sense of urgency will be fostered, however, a time will come when a plan will be required for the actual run. Obviously, this time will come closer to race day because by then, many of the initial complexities will be resolved. The general issues of marathon running will have been addressed and the overall complexity of the goal reduced. As with our 5K, on race day, complexity will have been reduced to the minimum and all that will remain is the requirement to act.

This is the basic *stair step* pattern involved in dealing with both increasing and decreasing goal complexities. As goals become more complex, the planning requirement increases. On a continuum it moves from simple *performance* (run) to devising an *implementation plan* (how to run a particular race), to a *plan about the goal* in general (training for a marathon a year away). And they work the same way back down. The stair steps reflect the essential drive for specificity. The chances for success will always increase, as the general is made specific.

The Plan

We started this discussion by claiming that every goal contained a nascent plan. That's because at the simplest performance level, knowing where you want to be and the criteria for success is the only plan you need. As goal complexity increases so does plan complexity. The world is filled with elaborate systems, but only four elements are required for a plan.

The *first element* is the *goal*. Every plan should be based on the type of *Fifth Station* goals we've been discussing. There should be a clear motive followed by the focus of a specific, measurable outcome. As noted, when complexity increases, so does the need for interim goals. These interim steps should be specifically timed and accompanied by achievement criteria. Related to this concept is the need for *deadlines*. While most people groan at the mere thought of deadlines, we know from long experience that they are vital.

At issue is the *planning fallacy*. The planning fallacy recognizes the well-established pattern of individuals and teams underestimating their own completion times, but not the completion times of others. This is the result of a selective application of experience. When looking at someone else's project, the team invariably is able to predict cases of over optimism based on their own previous experience. However, despite this keen insight, they typically ignore experience—even their own—when making projections about their completion times. Instead, they focus only on planning data to determine projected completion times and, as any *other* team could tell them, they tend to be overly optimistic. The planning fallacy is so common that it seems almost frighteningly genetic. Everyone can relate to the maddening last minute rush to get something done. Ubiquitous as it is, there is only one known cure—deadlines. Make them a part of your up-front planning.

The *second major plan element* is *operations*. This is the part of the plan where you describe how you plan to accomplish the goal. This is the strategy part of the plan. Again, there are many different approaches. The Quality Improvement Process, the Six Step Problem Solving Process, Strength Weakness, Opportunity and Threat Analysis; PERT, CPM, SPM, to name a few. The approach is less important than the fact that your plan has an appropriate methodology to achieve the desired end.

The process should include a means of determining the facts, uncovering the implications of the facts, an objective system of analysis and an evaluation of support and commitment.

The *third plan element* is *logistics*. Logistics is a broad category that focuses on acquiring and managing all the resources required for the project. These might be strictly material *resources*, such as running shoes, shorts and a T-shirt for our runner. Logistics might also involve hiring a coach for developmental purposes or covering travel arrangements. Logistics includes managing team *activities* as well. Work routines, meetings, schedules, deadlines all have to be coordinated and this is the part of the plan where such considerations are made.

The *fourth element* is *communications*. This is a critical, yet oft neglected area. Of course, if the plan is for an individual working alone, communications will be straightforward. When dealing with teams, however, complexity reigns. The communication plan should first establish individual roles and rules of engagement (accountability). The plan should also consider how work will be delegated, information synthesized and decisions made. Importantly, the preferred forms of media should be clearly established. Will e-mail be used instead of snail mail? What will be put on the intra-net? What software will be used? When will the team meet and for what reasons? Addressing these concerns up front will greatly streamline work processes throughout the project.

And that's the planning story. Plans are essential to achieving goals. From simple performance plans to detailed strategies about the nature of the goal itself, plans maximize the potential for success. Whether scaling Everest, walking up Fuji or running your first 5K, plans make it happen. In fact, a recent study demonstrated that planning increased the likelihood of goal attainment by 300%. But remember: *people don't spontaneously plan.* Particularly when under time pressure, they tend to rush headlong into operations despite the clear benefits of even simple planning. The challenge is to take the time. The benefits will follow.

The Success Effect

There is a final aspect of motivation that should be mentioned. It, too, can be expressed in an equation: $S = M^2$. That is, *Success* equals *motivation to the second power.* We know that the direct experience of success is the most effective way to promote confidence. It's also a phenomenally effective motivator. The reason for this is that *success is generative*. The experience of success increases the desire for success. It's a motivational opiate. This is the secret weapon of the card shark, who lets his mark win in order to feed the desire. Success at the game increases the desire to play and continue to win. The card shark then begins to beat the mark. This engages the risk-seeking behavior for loss as the mark desperately tries to win back his losses.

Fortunately, team success is far more benign. Team success impacts both individual and group motivation. It increases individual effort and, like accountability, promotes complex thinking among the whole team. Success fosters long lasting resiliency and commitment to team objectives. The result is that while motivation increases after a success, it does not necessarily decrease following a failure. Success leads individuals to rate their confidence high, and to evaluate the team as highly confident.

Success and rewards are closely linked. At one end of the continuum, there is intrinsic reward. People just "feel good" following a success. On the other end, rewards are directly linked to total compensation. At this end, livelihoods depend on successful task accomplishment. Underlying the entire continuum, however, is a single dynamic. Motivation is sustained and even enhanced, to the extent that performance is associated with valued outcomes. This is why an individual may be satisfied with just "feeling good" following volunteer work in their community, but would feel legitimately cheated that if instead of a pay check at the end of the month, they received only a hearty "thank you" from their employer.

Dissatisfaction develops when people believe their contributions are of greater value than the organizational rewards. This dissatisfaction is, of course, a significant de-motivator. Even when someone believes they can succeed at the task, they are less likely to even try if there is no clear association between performance and outcomes. Rewards must match performance, and once again, the team maker should clearly establish the reward structure prior to the team's initial assembly.

Rewards should be well thought out and care should be taken to ensure that they support the organization's overall mission. One organization that depended on the regular presence of their employees in the work place routinely gave time off as a reward for superior performance. While the workers positively perceived this, it sent the wrong message by placing a high value on behavior that was the exact opposite of what the organization desired.

Motivation actually *increased* when rewards were designed that supported the mission. Off-site training, use of lap top computers and direct Internet access turned out to be rewards enthusiastically received and held longer lasting positive effects while supporting the aim of having people regularly come to work. Certainly, incentive pay, cash bonuses, better work assignments are all possible tools that can be used to reward performance.

The best rewards, however, will be those valued by the worker. Any formal reward system should be supported by the constant celebration discussed as a part of building confidence. Ongoing celebration of positive events promotes motivation as it builds confidence.

The potency of success should never be underestimated. The experience of success within the team contributes to a sense of personal confidence, beliefs about the group's ability, general satisfaction, and organizational loyalty. People like to be winners, and they like to associate with winners. Success breeds success. It's an exponential motivator.

Because It's There

In 1922, George Mallory and a team of climbers made the first serious attempt to scale Everest. Back in England, Mallory was asked why he would undertake such a challenge. "Because it's there," came his reply.

Just as the climbing elite continues to pursue Everest and thousands of pilgrims approach Fuji "because it's there," teams will continue to advance on their objective, "because it's there." That is motivation at the *Fifth Station*.

We started with the great DNA stew of *dissonance, accountability* and *urgency*. We brought focus to the motive by making the outcomes of our desire *specific* and *measurable*. We realized 300% gains by judiciously applying *plans* as our goal complexity increased. We recognized the exponential motivating power of *success, reward and celebration*. And that's how Hillary made it all the way up the mountain and all the way back down again.

Decision-making

"Houston…"

President Kennedy decided. His advisors were deeply divided, but Kennedy was convinced. In an address to Congress on May 25, 1961, he issued the challenge:

> "I believe this nation should commit itself to achieving the goal, before the decade is out, of landing a man on the moon and returning him safely to earth. No single space project in this period will be more impressive to mankind, or more important for the long-range exploration of space, and, none will be so difficult or expensive to accomplish."

Kennedy's announcement came twenty days after Alan Shepard became the first American in space—and fifty-three days after Soviet cosmonaut Yuri Gagarin became the first man, not only to enter space, but to actually orbit the planet as well. Ever since the Soviets beat America into space with Sputnik in October of 1957, a race had been run between the two countries. The Soviets appeared to be way out ahead and virtually unstoppable. Now President Kennedy had thrown down the gauntlet for the biggest prize of them all—the moon.

On July 20, 1969 the goal was about to be reached. Traveling in lunar orbit, 389,645 kilometers from earth, astronauts Neil Armstrong and Buzz Aldrin received the final "Go," for the Lunar Module Eagle's powered descent to the moon. They were 192 miles from their touchdown point and exactly 50,174 feet above the surface. At the heart of Eagle was a computer that near instantaneously measured speed, velocity, rate of deceleration, thrust, height, angle of descent, fuel consumption, weight, balance and dozens of other vital factors. At this critical juncture, data rushed like water from a fire hose into the furiously working CPU. The computer would make a soft landing possible. The computer would enable the astronauts to again lift off. The computer would get them back to earth. And with the lunar surface fast approaching, the computer began to show signs of distress.

A yellow caution light blinked on, six thousand feet above the moon. Almost directly above the Eagle, in the Command Module, Columbia, Michael Collins received word from Armstrong, "Program Alarm. It's a 12-0-2." The 12-0-2 alarm signaled an *executive overflow*. An executive overflow means that the computer is receiving more information than it can process. In this case, the computer was operating on a one-second cycle. Every second, the computer calculated everything necessary for a soft landing as well as for an abort. The alarm was its way of saying, "enough is enough."

Though NASA's Apollo Project included, literally, a cast of thousands, there were only two individuals who knew enough about the on board computers to assess the program alarm: Steve Bales and Jack Garman. They were both in Mission Control. Bales functioned as the flight Guidance officer, or, GUIDO, and Garman was in a room next door. The two had personally programmed Eagle's computers and studied their performance in the course of countless simulations. Their knowledge went beyond sophistication to the profound. But now the Eagle was below six thousand feet and there was a 12-0-2. All eyes turned to Bales.

Before Gene Kranz, Apollo 8 Flight Director could ask the question, Bales had conferred with Garman. They thought they understood the problem. They thought that the hardware and software would continue to perform, but they wanted more data. But more data meant more time and time was now measured in *seconds*. Garman was confident that everything would be ok as long as there wasn't another program alarm. When Kranz asked, "GUIDO?" "Bales answered, "GO!"

But there were more 12-0-2's. At *five thousand* feet Kranz called for the final "GO—NO-GO." Bales was the last to answer. Despite the continuing alarms, Bales went with instinct and keyed in, "GO." He rode with his instinct when at *three thousand* feet there was another executive overflow alarm. He trusted instinct again at *two thousand* feet when the final alarm flashed across his monitor.

And his instinct had been right. The computer performed flawlessly— or almost flawlessly.

Somewhere in the vast network of calculations, a slight navigational error was about to make its presence felt. As Eagle began its final descent, thirteen hundred feet above the surface, Armstrong and Aldrin realized that they had overshot their landing point by four miles. With fuel critically low, Armstrong began to actually *fly* the Eagle and search out a new landing site. A level site was essential for a successful take off, but everywhere Armstrong looked, there were rocks, boulders and craters. With less than a minute's fuel remaining, he spotted a clearing and flew toward it. The following exchange comes from the actual space-to-ground tapes:

Eagle: 540 feet, down at 30 (feet per second)…down at 15…400 feet down at 9…forward 350 feet, down at 4…300 feet, down 3 1/2…47 forward…1 1/2 down…13 forward…11 forward. Coming down nicely…200 feet, 4 1/2 down…5 1/2 down…5 percent…75 feet…6 forward…lights on…down 2 1/2…40 feet? Down 2 1/2, kicking up some dust…30 feet, 2 1/2 down…faint shadow…4 forward…4 forward…drifting to right a little…O.K.…

Houston: 30 seconds (fuel remaining).

Eagle: Contact light! O.K., engine stop...descent engine command override off.

Houston: We copy you down, Eagle.

Eagle: Houston, Tranquility Base here. The Eagle has landed.

Decisions, Decisions, Decisions

Armstrong and Aldrin on the moon reflected the culmination of many decisions. Kennedy's initial decision was based, not on technological data, but on a desire to reinvigorate the New Frontier in the days following the ill-fated Bay of Pigs invasion. He saw a race for the moon as a way of energizing an entire nation. It reflected the way in which he valued courage and in the way he understood the human spirit.

As Eagle plunged toward the lunar surface, Bales and Garman made educated guesses about the on board computers. They played hunches on the strength of their detailed knowledge of the Lunar Module's hardware and software.

When Armstrong took control of Eagle he made split second decisions about the feel of his craft and the lay of the land. His every sense was alert as he piloted Eagle to a soft touchdown. These were different decisions, made by different individuals, toward a common end. Yet, in these decisions, we can discern what it takes to be successful. And successful decision-making begins with our original three principles: *WYSINWYG, Balance, and Simplicity*.

When Armstrong piloted the Eagle to the lunar surface, he made split second decisions on the basis of his logical analysis of the sensory data he was received as he flew. Armstrong's style is common among administrators, production workers and applied scientists.

Another decision-making style casts the nets wide. It seeks out the possibilities and then applies a structure to them. The system is always more interesting than the details. Bales and Garman were making decisions using this style when they assessed the 12-0-2 program alarms. They didn't have time to gather data, so they made reasoned decisions based on the theoretical capabilities of the on-board computers. Managers, lawyers and engineers often reflect this style.

Yet another style of decision-making looks at the big picture and finds the values in it. This is often the inspirational stuff of vision. Looking nine years out, Kennedy used this style when he announced the objective of going to the moon. At the time, it wasn't known with certainty that our technology would permit such an effort, but when he said, "We choose to go to the moon, not because it is easy, but because it is hard," he struck a resonant chord in the American people. He tapped the spirit of a nation that valued innovation, challenge and hard work. Clergy, artists and psychologists often use this style.

There is one final style. These decision-makers realistically assess the here and now and determines the immediate impact on people. They strive to provide service or satisfy a need. Interestingly, Kennedy used this style as well when he announced the mission to the moon. With the nation losing confidence in his administration, he needed something that would impact people now. He needed something for tomorrow's newspaper. Salesmen, teachers and social service workers frequently reflect this style.

These four decision-making styles are based on various means of gathering data. This chart shows the possible combinations. Armstrong was an ST as he piloted the Eagle. His decisions were practical and immediately applicable. Bales and Garman were operating in the NT style. Their systematic understanding of the theoretical helped them make sound decisions. Kennedy was in the NF quadrant when he electrified the public with his vision. He was also in the SF quadrant when he framed his vision in a way that gave public confidence in his administration an immediate boost.

Decision-making Style

	Sensing	*Intuition*
T h i n k i n g	Practical Application *ST*	Theoretical Design *NT*
F e e l i n g	Immediate Impact on People *SF*	Conceptual Value *NF*

The key to using the model is to begin with your *strength*. Gather data and draw conclusions in your *preferred* style first, then filter that view by examining it from the perspective of the other three styles. Your first filter should be data gathered in your *non-preferred function*, but evaluated in your *preferred* method of decision-making. Thus, an *NT* would first filter their view through the *ST* style.

Continue to cycle through the matrix to consider the other styles. In this way you'll cover all possible dimensions of a problem and greatly enhance your chances for making a good decision. For example, if you were an *NT*, you would begin your decision-making process in the upper right hand quadrant. You might logically consider the theoretical implications posed by the problem and think through possible solutions. Using the model, you would next be sure that you had gathered sufficient details about the problem and then conducted a realistic evaluation *(ST)*. Armed with the big picture as well as the particulars, you would next consider the immediate impact of the possible solution on the people involved *(SF)*. Finally, the possible solution should be studied in terms of our values. Does the solution reflect who we really are and what we really believe? Will it promote success by fostering harmony *(NF)*?

When cycling through the styles, remember that each has its own unique point of view and thus, poses its own set of questions. The ST decides on the basis of utility and fact. The ST asks, *"Is it practical? Can we actually do it?"* The NT decides by applying structure to the conceptual. The NT asks, *"Should we do it? Is it the best possible alternative?"* The NF decides by applying values across a wide spectrum. The NF asks, *"Does it reflect what we believe? Will it bring us together?"* Finally, the SF decides by assessing the impact on people now. The SF asks, *"Will it satisfy our immediate needs. Will it work for us right now?"*

For Example…

Let's see how one management team used the model to make the best possible decision. The company was a 100-bed residential behavioral treatment center for adolescents. The teens usually remained at the center for twelve months during which time they were assigned to one twenty-bed cottage. The treatment center was located in an area with many similar treatment facilities. Thus, competition was keen for a relatively fixed number of residents. Recently, the center had been operating at 60% capacity and was barely breaking even. At this point, even a slight drop in census would prove financially catastrophic. The management team (the *first tier* team) had a distinct *ST* flavor. After lively deliberation they proposed the following: immediately close two cottages (transfer those residents to vacant beds in other cottages), lay off the 24 direct care staff members associated with those cottages, eliminate the art, music and occupational therapy programs (6 professional staff members), replace those professional with one recreation therapist who would coordinate cottage based recreation programs. The beauty of the plan was that in addition to staving off financial ruin, it would actually provide some cushion until the small, but able marketing team could generate new contracts. The ST filter had produced a plan that was practical, doable, and that would resolve the immediate problem.

The plan was appealing, but the administrator decided to run it through an *NT* filter. Because the management team was so pleased with their plan, the administrator wanted to broaden the perspective and so commissioned a *second tier* team to help out. This team included people from all the departments at the center. The second tier team was charged to "think outside the box" and explore *all* possibilities. The final results exceeded all expectations.

Though highly creative, all the proposed ideas were well thought out and generally plausible. Interestingly, they recognized that the problems faced by the center were not unique. The entire industry was undergoing a major shakeout. They reasoned that the survivors would be those who offered stellar services at a competitive price. Thus, they ruled out any option that would diminish their unusual array of ancillary therapies.

Rather than eliminate the art, music and occupational therapy programs, they suggested becoming a therapy service provider organization. In this way, they could market the therapists' excess capacity to area schools, social service agencies and perhaps, to other treatment centers as well. A collateral benefit of this strategy would be the development of a broad referral base.

They also considered running alternative programming in some of the facilities excess physical plant capacity. An after school program for "at risk" teens was one suggestion that seemed especially promising. Finally, they proposed that the administration partner with the therapists to create internships at the center. An internship program could extend the staff at little or no cost.

The downside was that putting the plans into effect would take precious time and the revenues wouldn't fully offset the financial problems associated with low census. The NT filter proved most valuable in generating *different approaches* to the problem, and shifting the focus from cutting *costs* to generating *income*.

Generally pleased, the administrator decided to apply the *NF* filter. This step engendered some real soul searching as both teams thoughtfully reviewed why they were in the business to begin with. They asked what they were trying to accomplish on behalf of the residents placed in their care. They reviewed their vision statement and treatment philosophy. In the end, both teams agreed that gutting the treatment program would violate everything they valued about helping troubled youths. They reaffirmed that the center had to be a safe, treatment focused home for their residents. It also had to be a creative, dynamic environment for both the professional and direct-care staff.

Everyone seemed a little surprised at what they had learned during the review. Certainly it wasn't anything new, but in the press of daily events they realized they had lost a sense of their greater purpose in this important profession. They rediscovered that their outcomes were measured in *changed lives* rather than *filled beds*. The NF filter helped reaffirm the center's greater purpose. It helped the teams avoid the danger of piece mealing away the things that originally made their program unique and beneficial.

The administrator pressed bravely forward and had the teams examine their options through the *SF* filter—and what a filter it was! The immediate human impact was profound no matter which way they turned. First of all, closing two units would wreak havoc with every resident in the center. Each cottage reflects a carefully nurtured environment. It was a family oriented therapeutic milieu in which the bulk of individual learning took place. Transferring residents from one unit to another would fundamentally change the character of every cottage. If this occurred at the same time that staff were cut back, the only certainty would be that no one would be getting better for a long, long time. Of course, letting that many staff go all at once would be devastating to them individually. The market was already contracting and the likelihood of finding work was slim. Those remaining would be assuming substantially more responsibility with a correspondingly decreased sense of job security. Just watch for the WYSINWYG implications here!

The SF filter helped the teams recognize that the human impact of the plan might outweigh the benefits. If treatment was severely compromised, the sponsoring agencies might very well pull their residents form the center. The teens needed stability more than they needed anything and the SF filter demonstrated the extent to which that would be lost in the whirl-wind of transfers, closings and layoffs.

At this point, the management team revisited the issue in its entirety. They decided that any discussion had to be framed from the perspective of their treatment values. They were, after all, in the helping profession. Making kids better was why they were there to begin with. But their hard-nosed look at the financial and market situation convinced them that their treatment program would have to change.

It was unlikely that sponsoring agencies would ever have enough money to pay for all the services the center would like to provide. Since public agencies would be unable to completely underwrite the center's programming, the team decided to create new avenues for generating revenues. Their new plan accomplished their goals, but did so in a way that reflected *progress* rather than retrenchment.

The team began by doing a cottage-by-cottage resident case review. They found that one cottage had a census of only eight and that four of the eight were about to be discharged. As the remaining four residents were relatively new to the center, the clinical staff felt they could be comfortably transferred to another cottage. The team decided to temporarily close this cottage when the residents were discharged.

In order to reduce staff costs, they changed the staff to resident ratio from 1:5 to 1:6. Eliminated positions would be dealt with through attrition. Staff members were also offered an opportunity to transfer to the float pool. They would be guaranteed 20 hours a week at a slightly higher hourly rate. Taking advantage of an immediate local need, the closed cottage would be slightly remodeled and open as an "at risk" day program. The team also began aggressively marketing the services of the ancillary therapists and partnered with the State University to participate in internship programs.

Applying the four styles helped the team stay faithful to their individual and corporate values. It encouraged them to look beyond the immediate crisis and develop strategies that would take care of the immediate needs and that would position themselves for a successful future. They were also able to develop a strategy that minimized any negative impact on residents' and staff. Importantly, the plan sent a message to *all* involved, that they were individually important to the center.

The best decisions will always be made when all four styles are consulted. The consultation need not be elaborate and time consuming. It should be only enough to provide a *balanced* perspective. Failing to take account of both the *facts* and *possibilities* of a situation puts blinders on decision-making. Failing to weigh data both *objectively* and *subjectively* produces lopsided and often inefficient solutions to pressing problems.

The Anatomy of a Team Decision

Up to this point, we've been discussing the *nature* of decision-making. We gather information and then make judgments about that information. This is true whether we are making personal or team decisions. We begin with our own style, and then apply the other three styles to a problem or issue. This optimizes our decision-making by ensuring that we examine the issue from all possible perspectives. But team decision-making brings a whole new set of complexities.

For one thing, all four decision-making styles might be represented on a seven-member team. Harmonizing the different views takes both thought and time. WYSINWYG will also be a factor. Seven people on a team will initially bring seven different senses of priority, commitment and urgency. Again, thought and time will be required to bring the entire team to the same level of understanding. These and other complexities require that teams pay careful attention to the three-part structure of a team decision.

Let's start with the actual decision point. A wide range of data has been gathered and both objectively and subjectively analyzed. It's time to choose, and you do. Is that it? Has the decision been reached? Can we go home now? Not yet.

The decision point is really just the *burger on the bun*. It's literally sandwiched between two equally important elements in the process of reaching a final decision. The decision point is always preceded by your *first impressions*. These impressions derive from your data-gathering and from your previous experience with the subject. Often first impressions will determine the outcome of your final decision because they'll shape how you assemble and analyze the information to begin with.

Next element in the anatomy of a decision is the *decision point* itself and is produced as the result of *active discussion*. This is the culminating point of your efforts. It may occur entirely in your own mind for a personal decision or in a team's primary forum, the *meeting*. Meetings are an incredibly dynamic forum and reflect WYSINWYG and Chaos at their utmost. They are WYSINWYG in that more is always going on than meets the eye and chaotic in that there are profound behavioral paradigms active just out of sight.

The final element of the anatomy is *second thoughts*. Second thoughts refer to the ideas, attitudes and opinions that you have following the decision point. Just because you've reached a decision doesn't mean you'll stick to it. Second thoughts run from, *"I wish I'd said..."* to the notorious *"buyer's remorse."* The extent to which first impressions and active discussion are effectively managed will determine the magnitude of second thoughts. The good news is that each of these three elements can not only be managed, but when the underlying paradigms are recognized and employed, extraordinary results will follow.

First Impressions

The focus of this element, *first impressions*, in on the individual. Every team begins as an aggregate of individuals. Before any meeting, whether face-to-face, on-line or video, you form *impressions* about what will be expected of you and the possible outcomes of the exchange. These impressions will determine how you prepare for the meeting.

At one extreme, you won't prepare at all. Your impression might be that nothing will be expected and that you won't have to immediately respond to anything. Let's face it; most routine business meetings are like this. The boss holds a weekly meeting whether it's needed or not. He or she talks for an hour, does a "roundtable" during which everyone passes and then adjourns. Your mind is on *cruise control* and you're secretly learning to sleep with your eyes open.

The other, more terrifying extreme is when you're called in to defend your project against organized criticism. Now you're in *overdrive* and adrenaline has your synapses snap, crackle and poppin' like a bowl of Rice Krispies. Obviously, if you expect to be in the hot seat, you'll show up well prepared and in an asbestos suit.

Shaping first impressions results from our personal commitment and our expectations about the commitment of the other team members to the subject at hand. The relationship between these factors will largely determine your degree of preparation and the way in which you'll participate in the active discussion. The next table displays the four basic approaches to active discussion that will result from your individual first impressions.

Personal Commitment

	Strongly Committed	*Uncommitted*
A w a r e	Fixed	Easy Agreement
U n a w a r e	Persuasive	Flexible

Easy Agreement results when you have no particular commitment to the topic of the meeting and pretty much know how the others feel. Whether or not *they* are strongly committed or completely uncommitted, the driving factor is *your* lack of commitment. If you know the others feel strongly about a subject and you don't, you're likely to go along with whatever they want to do. It's no big deal. It's also not a big deal if you don't care and they don't care. The result will be the same—*easy agreement*.

It relates back to our principle of *balance*. Without some force that pushes to the extremes, people will naturally gravitate to the center. Easy agreement simply means that without investing much time or thought, everyone's comfortable with the possible outcome. Not surprisingly, this is the case with most routine meetings and it's not necessarily a bad position. Time is always at a premium. If everyone took time to carefully study the routine, there would be little time left to consider the critical. Easy agreement is an effective way to quickly dispatch the mundane.

But it can create problems. The shadow side of easy agreement is *complacency*. Complacency occurs when you are *content* with the status quo and *lose* your WYSINWYG ability to anticipate both opportunities and threats. Microsoft's anti-trust problem began with their failure to initially recognize the Internet's impact. By the time they saw the opportunity, a small, but robust industry had taken root. Microsoft's aggressive efforts to catch-up were ultimately seen as anti-competitive.

Complacency also occurs when people *don't believe their voice will be heard*. After all, why take a stand when the team will do what it wants to anyway. This view is often manifested when people decide to tell the boss what the boss wants to hear. It's also the source of many *second thoughts* that may later scuttle a decision on which the team believed they had reached consensus.

A final problem with complacency is that it can lead to everyone agreeing to do something that *no one* really wants to do. Without a particular preference for one course over another, members of the team agree to actions to which they believe the others are committed. Of course if no one on the team has a preference, a decision will be reached through a series of vague agreements. Without realizing it, the focus of the team shifts from *goal orientated* decision-making to team *harmony*. No matter what the reason, complacency is anathema to good decision-making.

Probably the best way to manage easy agreement is to stop having meetings to discuss the *routine*. Because such meetings predominate in so many organizations, they create a culture in which easy agreement generalizes to *all* meetings. Routine subjects can best be dealt with through mediums such as e-mail. It's a quick and dynamic way to get the word out. It's also wise to *publish agendas* beforehand that clearly *state expectations* of participants. If you're just passing information, say that, but if you want team members to do more than just listen, shape that expectation in advance.

An excellent means of avoiding complacency is to encourage *contrarian* input. By no means does this mean disagreement simply for the sake of disagreement. That kind of behavior produces nothing but frustration, wasted time, and a profound "urge to kill" among team members. Rather, it means *creating opportunities* and then *positively recognizing* those who challenge assumptions with plausible alternatives. This can be accomplished electronically: "Please e-mail me four projects that you would like to work on, if your division wasn't fully committed to Project X. We'll look over everyone's input at our next weekly staff meeting." Or, "contrarian" meetings could be scheduled on a regular basis. The goal is simply to look at the routine with a fresh set of eyes. It could be that easy agreement was well earned or it could just mean that an exciting new challenge might emerge. If done consistently, such opportunities will establish an organizational culture in which innovation is an integral part of routine decision-making. The contrarian approach also demonstrates the second of our first impression quadrants.

When you are personally uncommitted to a subject or course of action and you are unaware of the other team members' commitment, you tend to remain *flexible*. Before the meeting, you are likely to think about the topic and develop alternatives that might prove acceptable to everyone. In essence, you're *establishing a point of view*. This process marks the initial stirrings of personal accountability. Even though you are uncommitted at this point, there is the potential that you'll have to take a stand when you learn how the others feel about the topic.

On one hand you night find yourself in easy agreement, but you may just as likely find yourself in opposition. Until you have a clearer sense of the other's positions, you'll pay closer attention to the facts, weigh them against possibilities and look for potential pitfalls among the likely alternatives. Though you're doing some analytical work, because you are basically uncommitted, the outcome you desire is flexibility. You're looking for the range of alternatives that you could support. This approach is often triggered when you're invited to a meeting to discuss a problem that you or your department isn't experiencing. It may also be triggered when you are part of a team evaluating a project that won't directly task you for performance. You assume that your role in such meetings is that of consultant.

Flexibility is almost always a beneficial approach. Because it engenders *accountability* and thus fosters *complex thinking*, a full range of alternatives can be identified and evaluated. Without commitment to any particular alternative, there is less chance for parochial attachments to cloud the decision-making process. Yet this strength can hide a weakness. The lack of commitment can sometimes translate into a lack of *urgency*.

Without a sense of urgency, the subject can become just one of many. It may not be viewed as important enough to warrant too much consideration. Without some sense of passion about the outcome, the search for good alternatives may produce nothing more than an adequate solution that offends no one, rather than a challenging outcome that pushes the team's capabilities. In the business lexicon, this approach, at its worst, produces the nefarious *"committee decision."* The committee decision selectively breeds out ingenuity through a complex network of compromises. In the end, all that is left is a well-crafted decision—amazing only for its mediocrity.

The set backs with this approach are, however, small compared with the benefits. It was this kind of thinking that led Ford's team to consider such disparate facilities as meat packing plants and grain elevators as prototypes for their assembly line. The master inventor, Thomas Edison and his team of assistants followed this process when they tested thousands of filaments for thirteen months before identifying the one that would literally illuminate the world. They searched for the *best* solution, not *a* solution.

Fostering this approach is relatively easy to do. It's as simple as applying the DNA of motivation. You'll recall that we said motivation equals dissonance plus accountability, multiplied by urgency. To apply this DNA in developing a flexible first impression, alert the participants to the gap between where you are and where you want to be. That is, alert them to the meeting's purpose and desired outcome. Next tell them what will be *expected* in terms of participation. Finally, set *deadlines* that establish the project's *importance* and *urgency*. The following memo, announcing a meeting to review and act on administrative cost overruns covers all these bases.

TO: Department Heads

FROM: VP Administrative Services

Since the beginning of the fiscal year we've been experiencing administrative cost overruns in many departments. I'm open to all suggestions, but we have to get back on track.

I've scheduled a meeting on Wednesday at 9:00 AM to identify possible solutions. I'd like to leave that meeting with at least a preliminary game plan. In order to make the most of our time together, please identify any overruns in your department and draft a brief explanatory paragraph. Additionally I'd like everyone to identify three possible ways of bringing our budget back in line. To paraphrase the car dealers, "No reasonable suggestion refused!"

Please e-mail this information to me by close of business tomorrow so that I can consolidate your input for the meeting.

The memo provides all the ingredients necessary to promote flexible thinking. If your department isn't experiencing any overruns this is basically an exercise in creative planning. If, however, your department is responsible for some or most of the problem, you'll undoubtedly recognize that you're about to receive a lot of advice. If you have strong opinions about the overruns and want to shape your own destiny, you'll probably engage in some first impression, third quadrant thinking.

If you're strongly committed to an idea, yet are unaware of the other team members commitment, you'll likely prepare for active discussion by developing *persuasive arguments*. This first impression approach is very similar to the last. It relies on the same motivational aspects of dissonance, accountability and urgency that developing flexible alternatives did. Now, however, the intensity has increased because you are strongly committed to a particular point of view. Thus, your sense of *accountability is pronounced* because of your responsibility for the outcome. If you want to prevail, you'll have to convince the others.

Of course, since you are as yet unaware of the others' preferences, you may discover that they are in easy agreement with you. That approach, however, entails risk. Rather, you are more likely to craft *possible arguments* in your favor. You'll *anticipate objections* and *prepare counter arguments* as well. Though engaging in the same kind of complex thinking as when flexibility was the aim, now there is a sense of doggedness in your preparations. The goal is no longer to determine which option among many you can support, but how can you persuade the team to *your* point of view.

There are many reasons why you might find yourself using this approach. In the previous example, if you were responsible for the overruns, you might want to persuade the team that they were legitimate and self-correcting. This approach is also common when you're pitching a new idea or trying to make a contrarian case that is of real importance to you. It's also the heart and soul of sales. You may be pitching *solutions* to a client, but your solutions are all in *your* product line. Few salesmen help clients find flexible alternatives that don't ultimately promote a sale.

The shadow side of this approach is easy to spot. Pushing a particular point of view can blind you to other, better alternatives. It can make you ignore contradictory warnings that might cause failure in the long run. It also provides less room for compromise, leading to defensiveness and in some cases, fostering confrontational meetings. If you don't prevail, it can produce disappointment that may undermine the chosen course of action. This of course, will be revealed in the kind of second thoughts that keep a decision from being fully supported.

But the shadow should not conceal the value of this approach. A passionate commitment to an idea or course of action is often what drives *progress*. It's also the means by which values can be effectively asserted in the face of "facts." This is just the approach used by Juror No. 8 (Henry Fonda) in Sidney Lumet's 1957 landmark film, *12 Angry Men*. After the first ballot, eleven jurors let out a weary sigh of resignation and begin to review the evidence in the face of one dissenting vote. It's ultimately Juror No. 8's thoughtful persuasiveness that moves them to a conclusion that none had expected. Success is often born of such persuasiveness.

Leaders can foster persuasiveness by using the same motivational DNA formula used to develop flexible thinking by *increasing the accountability*. An individual responsible for an outcome will use all the persuasiveness in his arsenal to make his case.

In the above memo a slight change in the addressee would create the desired result. If "Mr. Werquer" was tasked to develop and present a solution rather than the Department Heads, you can bet his preparation would be both thorough and convincing. (Although the other attendees might approach the meeting with easy agreement.)

If time and resources permit, assigning two or more individuals or teams to propose a solution can produce excellent results. Competitiveness is a natural outgrowth of this approach and can be highly motivating. Leaders, if fostering this approach, should be particularly sensitive to the pitfalls. Solid guidelines for team citizenship should be in place to avoid defensiveness and nonproductive arguing.

Team members should understand that progress comes from both the misses and the hits. Everyone should remember that no matter who carries the banner for a particular cause, the net result will be a *team* decision. The revised memo is a good way to promote persuasive arguments in a positive manner.

TO: Mr. Werquer

FROM: VP Administrative Services

Since the beginning of the fiscal year we've been experiencing administrative cost overruns in many departments. I'm open to all suggestions, but we have to get back on track.

I've scheduled a meeting on Wednesday at 9:00 AM to identify possible solutions. I'd like to leave that meeting with a game plan. Because of your special expertise, I'd like you to develop a draft solution for this problem and formally present it to the management team. Take a hard look at the overruns in all the departments and come up with what you believe will be the best strategy for getting us back on target.

Make your proposal as comprehensive as possible, but consider it a draft. I'll circulate it to other Department heads before the meeting and we can hash out the final solution after your presentation. I know I'm giving you the biggest part of this assignment, but we might as well put the other folks to work as well.

Consider this your top priority and have your draft to me by close of business Monday.

This memo should trigger all the elements necessary to produce a productive discussion on the overruns. It will result in a thorough presentation by Mr. Werquer while keeping the other Department heads engaged. Of course, if Mr. Werquer becomes too enamored of his proposal, he may find himself visiting the final first impression quadrant.

If you're strongly committed to an idea or course of action and you are aware of the other members' commitment, your approach to active discussion is likely to be *fixed*. It doesn't matter if you agree or disagree with the other members; *the principle consideration is your point of view.* Should your view coincide with the other members, the result is usually *mutually reinforcing* discussion. That is, everyone will engage in behavior that validates the common belief. Information held in common will be considered most reliable and new information is admitted to discussion only if it comes from a trusted source.

In cases where your opinion differs from that of other team members, the result is often stalemated discussion. The differing opinions need not be diametrically opposed for stalemate to ensue. In some cases differences are only a matter of degree, but the zealous adherence to only one option keeps team members from consensus. In this approach the time before a discussion is spent consolidating a position. All defenses are marshaled until your opinion seems unassailable.

Certainly, this is the most problematic of the first impression approaches because even at its best, it shuts down discussion. People who simply agree to disagree are not likely to make progress toward a goal. People who spend time in mutually reinforcing meetings are also unlikely to do more that perpetuate the status quo. This approach discourages *complex thinking* and promotes what is commonly called stubbornness, rigidity and bull headedness! Unfortunately, it's also a mainstay of American mythology.

In song, story, film and video, the image of the rugged individual standing tall in the face of all opposition has become the stuff of legend. Of course, the lone individual is always proven right by the time the credits roll. And there *are* times when adhering to your position in the face of all obstacles is the right thing to do.

When it comes to *values, principles, safety and the law,* the best approach is to hold fast to what you know is right. More than once, organizations have slowly, almost imperceptibly slipped into making decisions that they later regretted because they violated their values. In hindsight the errors seemed clear, but at the time no one spoke up in opposition (everyone just went along in easy agreement).

The mental health field has been plagued by such problems throughout its history. In recent years State sponsored investigations in New Jersey, Florida and Texas revealed numerous problems with illegal commitments. Rarely were the practitioners involved following criminal ends. Instead, they were well-intentioned individuals whose zeal for providing expedient treatment led them to overlook due process considerations.

Perhaps if more people had displayed *fixed beliefs* about the clinical and legal aspects of hospital commitment, the misjudgments would have never been able to take root. Mental health isn't alone in this regard. Almost everyday one hears of cover-ups, influence peddling and other unsavory acts that involve people who really do know better. They lose their moral and legal compass in the face of attractive and highly persuasive arguments. Again, adherence to fixed beliefs in such cases is not only desirable, but also mandatory. Team leaders should be certain that every member understands that values, principles, safety and the law are not subject to compromise. Those individuals who serve as the steady voice of team conscience should be celebrated at every opportunity. That said, rigid thinking on almost any other subject is never a good idea and it certainly won't enhance active discussion.

Shaping First Impressions

Personal Commitment	*Management Strategy*
Easy Agreement	- Don't meet for routine tasks - Publish agendas in advance - State clear expectations - Encourage contrarian views
Flexible	- Create dissonance - Focus expectations - Use deadlines to foster urgency
Persuasive	- Identify individual accountability - Apply motivational DNA
Fixed	- Display alternatives - Clarify non-negotiable items

A Final Caution

We've focused on how *first impressions* form and set the stage for active discussion from an individual perspective. Team leaders and members shouldn't lose sight of the fact that on a team of seven there might be two individuals with different points of view who plan to use persuasion to move the team. On the same team we might find one person with a fixed point of view that differs from that held by the persuaders. Three others seeking easy agreement may join them. A lone flexible thinker might then round out the team. This team will certainly have some interesting discussions on the way to their final decision.

The point to remember is that different members will bring with them different decision-making styles and different first impressions. None of this will be immediately apparent. Using the techniques suggested can mitigate some possible negative effects. Harder to manage is our assumption that our way is everyone's way. Keep WYSINWYG in mind. Concealed information can't be leveraged to produce a good decision. Thus, the first challenge of active discussion will be to *get first impressions on the table*.

Active Discussion

Magic time! *Active discussion* that produces a decision is what teams are all about. Yet as we've seen, by the time the team is seated around a table a host of complexities will have been encountered. We know that members will have their own *decision-making styles*. We know that the best decisions will be made after being filtered by all four styles. All four may be represented on the team, but more likely, the leader will have to assess what's missing and use the style matrix as a decision-making guide.

We also know that every member will form *first impressions* about the subject at hand. These range from, "I won't budge," to; "I don't care." Team leaders will have to shape member expectations before the meeting in order to promote complex thinking about the subject and flexibility.

The quality of both the meeting and the decision will also be impacted by the extent to which the team has been properly *assembled*. Ideally, the core team should have no more than five to seven members. The members should have a common understanding of the team's code of conduct. All members should know the goal and their individual responsibilities. Most importantly, teams should only meet to problem solve, coordinate or make decisions; and then, only if absolutely necessary.

With these elements in place, we can safely consider the dynamics of the discussion itself.

Consensus

Every team discussion should have a point. This may seem obvious, but in a crowd of a hundred, at least a hundred and one will concede that they've participated in many, many pointless discussions. The brave will acknowledge that most of their work-team discussions are pointless. Throughout the land, Mr. and Ms. Werquer's days are filled with an apparently endless series of meetings that seem to spontaneously generate. With each new promotion, the number of meetings you're expected to attend exponentially increases. Finally, one day, on the lonely ride home you realize that you'd been in meetings from eight to five and didn't seem to have accomplished anything. And so I repeat, every team discussion should have a *point.*

To truly test your capacity for surprise, we might extend that thought by adding that every team discussion should have a point that every member knows in *advance* and is *prepared* to achieve. The point may be a final decision. *"By the end of the meeting I want a definite rollout date."* It may also be tentative. *"Today we'll complete our draft proposal on next year's bonus plan. Take the draft back to your departments for comment and we'll finalize it at our Thursday meeting."* Sometimes the point will be to evaluate information that requires face-to-face interaction. *"I know that several team members have strong and conflicting opinions about the IPO. This meeting will give everyone an opportunity to air his or her point of view and field questions. We'll meet again next week to make a final decision."*

Whatever the point, it is an indispensable prerequisite of a meeting. And if the discussion is to produce consensus, the participants will have to know the point far enough in advance to *prepare* their first impressions thoroughly to make a *meaningful* contribution. The point is also the *dissonance* marker. It's what will alert the team members of the gap between the "as is" and the desired state. The point will make consensus possible because it will function as the target of the discussion. It will clarify what you want to reach consensus about.

But what exactly is *consensus*? The American Heritage Dictionary defines it as, "an opinion or position reached by a group as a whole or by majority will." The second definition of consensus is "general agreement or accord." The definition itself hints at what makes consensus so tricky. "Majority will," and "general agreement" aren't necessarily compatible concepts. The majority implies a minority. The minority might be the loyal opposition, a dissenting opinion or a disenfranchised member who'll never support the team decision. General agreement may be nothing more than passionless desires to keep everyone happy. True consensus is made of sterner stuff.

In one of the delightful ironies of human behavior, real consensus requires the fixed belief discussed in the fourth quadrant of our first impression matrix. Fixed beliefs were generally panned as an ineffective approach to active discussion. This kind of thinking before a discussion does nothing to develop a balanced understanding of each issue's aspects. But at the decision point, where consensus is required, it precisely defines the ideal condition.

Recall that the fourth quadrant reflects an individual with strong commitment and a full awareness of the commitment held by the other members. Consensus, then, would mean that each member strongly supports the decision and confidently knows that the other members strongly support it as well. Confirming this type of consensus is what Gene Kranz was doing in Mission Control when he polled each launch officer for a GO—NO-GO decision. Every member of the team had to strongly support the decision for a moon landing. Equivocation would mean that there were still loose ends. With two lives and the future of the manned space program in the balance nothing short of *full* and *transparent* commitment from every team member was required.

In the absence of this confident support, problems with *second thoughts* loom large. Though we'll discuss those in greater detail in the next section, it's worth noting now that awareness of mutual support is the best indicator that the issue has been thoroughly aired. If members are uncertain of where the others stand, it may mean that more persuading is required or that other options should be tested. If the individual isn't strongly committed, there is a good chance that their support will vacillate in the face of new data or outsider criticism. If you're not fully behind the decision, you'll be hard pressed to defend or explain it to those outside the team. Real consensus does not exist until there *is general agreement* that everyone can *fully* support the decision.

What happens if the team can't reach consensus? It depends. If the team was assembled to gather and organize data, there will be room enough for virtually all points of view. If the team was to submit a proposal, it might well be appropriate to forward a majority and minority report. If the results of the team effort produced two distinct products, the decision-makers would do well to evaluate the complexity of the issue and reevaluate the original goal for clarity. It may be more difficult than originally thought.

On the other hand, if the team was tasked to reach a single decision point or complete a specific mission, consensus will be the price of success. If the goal is to get everyone across the rain-swollen river, it won't suffice to leave one member behind because he couldn't support the team approach to stringing the lifeline. Instead, the team will have to continue the discussion and carefully identify competing arguments and *balance* them against potential solutions. If the *civics* of the team are established it will only be a matter of time before consensus is reached.

What We Know About Team Discussion

We have a *point* and *consensus* is the *goal*. Our next priority is to use what we know about team discussion to help reach our decision-making goal.

Probably the single greatest factor in team discussion is the relentless drive for *balance.* At their most elemental levels, teams move inexorably toward the mean. This movement spawns *four* powerful dynamics that shape team decisions independently of the content or goal of the discussion.

*The first dynamic of active discussion: **teams tend to prefer to discuss common knowledge rather than new information.*** This dynamic presents both an opportunity and a challenge. The opportunity is that teams will actively discuss and make decisions on the basis of their common pool of knowledge. Thus anything that makes it on the team's radar will have a chance of influencing an outcome. The challenge, of course, is that the data pool will be small and the team will make decisions on the basis of partial data.

As you might guess, *common knowledge* is the product of one's *decision-making style* and the *first impressions* formed before the discussion. The more homogeneous the team, the more likely that discussion will include and consider reliable information obtained in the preferred decision-making style. For example, a team of ST's is more likely to discuss factual data in a logical way. This will be considered the most *credible* approach. Theoretical data or subjective evaluation will be considered less reliable and may actually be discounted or ignored. Similarly, people with common decision-making styles will be attuned to information reflected by that style. Thus, it isn't surprising that our team of ST's will be likely to independently gather similar kinds of data and form similar first impressions. This information will be the *first revealed* by team members during the discussion.

Because of their similarities in approach, team members will be able to validate each other's opinions. With this validation, common knowledge is not only *discussed first, but at greater length* than new information. It will also be *repeated* more frequently. The net result is that the common knowledge receives strong confirmation. Common knowledge, then, is the data considered *credible* and *reliable* by the majority of the team. It is not necessarily data that everyone agrees with. Rather, common knowledge is data that is *team-validated* as worthy of examination.

Of course, new information can make its way into the common knowledge base. A member can successfully introduce innovative ideas or challenge team assumptions by establishing the credibility of new information through *persuasion*. Appealing to the decision-making styles of the majority best does this. Thus, an NT might suggest a new theoretical approach by demonstrating its practical applicability to the majority ST team members. Such appeals, however, require *persistence*. The tendency of the team will be to *discuss the new ideas less and repeat them fewer times*. The advocate must keep reasserting the new position for the team to consider it fully.

This pool of common knowledge can also be augmented through the input of *experts* or *prestigious* members. These represent the quickest way of exposing the team to new information with some certainty that it will be accepted. The expert operates with the aura of authority. If the team acknowledges this expertise, they will include the new information in their base of common knowledge. They'll discuss, repeat and award credibility on the basis of expert testimony. Prestigious members also carry disproportionate weight. Let's face it; if the Executive Vice President drops in on your meeting and encourages you to consider something new, chances are you will.

In addition to *hierarchical* status, prestige might derive from some *unique training* or *previous work* on a successful project. In either case, the team awards credibility on the basis of some credential that's considered valuable. Whether the credential derives from technical expertise or status, the team will be willing admit the new information to its knowledge base that might otherwise have been excluded.

Ultimately the success of the effort will depend on the extent to which the new information is *verified* by each member's *experience*. This relates to our earlier observation that a paradigm is unlikely to be replaced until it is found wanting and a new paradigm is discovered.

Once the new information is granted credibility by the team, it stands a good chance of shaping the outcome of the discussion.

There are *four discussion strategies* that teams can use to develop a productive pool of common knowledge. Common knowledge will be the basis for the discussion and therefore, establishing the pool is a vital first step.

The first strategy is to accept all ideas. Every effort should be made to get as much data in front of the team as possible. Conscious application of all four decision-making styles and careful management of first impressions can go a long way toward ensuring that all sides of an issue are considered. Data developed through this approach should be presented either *prior to or at the beginning* of the meeting. To the extent possible, the information should be provided to team members in *written* form.

Initially, *all information should be considered important.* Material that first appeared unpromising might become significant when additional information is brought to bear. Care should be taken not to filter out data too early in the process. The application of filters to rule out material should be self-consciously made by the team and always encompass all four decision-making styles.

The second strategy is to actively critique each idea. Team members often become hyper-civilized. (Though I am sure everyone can think of times when this was not the case!) They become reluctant to dispute an idea offered by another member or provide information that disputes an accepted norm. To reach an effective decision, however, it's important that all information is thoroughly evaluated. *Critical examination*, even if only done briefly, fosters *dissonance* and promotes the kinds of *complex thinking* that leads to excellent results. Sad to say, but true, the chief reason teams fail to evaluate thoroughly is the fear of *causing offense.*

Often people mistake critical examination of their ideas with a personal indictment of their abilities. As we've noted before, a team that are properly assembled and on which confidence has been promoted, will avoid this difficulty. It's also helpful to use a simple technique, such as Hegel's *dialectic* discussed in the chapter on balance as an evaluation device. Using the dialectic approach, each idea is clearly formulated, then analyzed for problems and a *synthesis* proposed.

The resulting synthesis will produce a stronger argument or will discredit the original idea. This system is simple and promotes balanced conclusions. It is important that the process be kept "honest." Too often, tired teams will say, "Well, the idea is so good, I can't think of any reason not to do it!" In this life you can be certain that while you may not see the problem, someone else will.

Critically examining new information is the third discussion strategy. Sometimes new information presented by prestigious or expert members can overwhelm the team and hijack the decision-making process. This happens when the team *uncritically awards credibility* to such data. After all, experts aren't always right (just consider market analysts), and frequently the input of high status members is misinterpreted. The annals of corporate America are littered with examples of random CEO speculations that magically turned into policy because, "it's what the boss wanted."

Particularly dangerous is new information presented as *"insider information."* Occasionally, a team member will attempt to give new information added authority by attributing it to behind the scene sources. This tends to erode confidence and guarantees that the team will never make a decision on the basis of the actual facts. Of course, as we've noted, there are many times when new information will be valuable and should become a part of the knowledge pool. The issue is that new data should never sway the group without critical examination. New information is only as good as common knowledge until demonstrated to be better.

The fourth discussion strategy is to display all data. A major difficulty during discussion is that information, once stated is often *lost or forgotten.* This is why common information is more frequently discussed and more often used as the basis for making decisions. Information known to only one or a few members is more readily *forgotten* and therefore not discussed. The simple consequence is that information that isn't a part of the discussion is not likely to be used to make the decision. For this reason, it's always helpful to record and publicize all the information produced by the team. Flip charts, meeting minutes or handouts will all accomplish this end. The only caution is that care should be taken to avoid heavy editing or editorializing by the scribe.

It's also a good idea to stop the progress of the discussion at intervals to *review* what has been said. While momentum shouldn't be sacrificed, it's important that all pertinent data be kept in the team's consciousness. These recaps need not be lengthy to be effective. A quick review of the discussion to that point may be all it takes to help intuitive information gatherers string some innovative ideas or for sensors to spot an overlooked fact.

The second dynamic of active discussion: teams perform better than their average member does, but worse than their best member does. This holds true for *operational* teams as well. The opportunity inherent in this dynamic is the recognition that teams, even without much conscious effort, will exceed the capacity of their average members. In general then, there is a *"dividend"* associated with the use of teams. The challenge is to leverage the additional expertise of the best member.

The difficulty is related to the problems of introducing new information to the team. The best members operate at the extreme edge of team capability. Not surprisingly, they are likely to have some information or a perspective that is not common to the group. The naturally tendency of the team will be to *marginalize* this information unless there is a direct effort to include it.

Failure to capitalize on all the available resources of the team means that outcomes are never really as good as they could be. We saw this when we noted that individuals working alone on a problem and then pooling their data produced between 100% and 400% more ideas than did a team meeting face-to-face. Obviously, the best way to correct for this dynamic is to be sure to use the right type of team for the right kind of task. We saw this demonstrated in the Great American Chopstick campaign. When *coordination*, *persuasion* and *subjective decision-making* are required, actively involving the best member and introverts is essential for effective team discussion.

The strategy of actively involving the "best" member and introverts requires the active efforts of the team or discussion leader. They must first identify the best member and then foster that member's participation. Care must be taken to identify the *best* member—not the most domineering member, or the most powerful, or prestigious, or most charismatic member. The best member is one who brings unusually rich skills, insights or information to the team.

Unless the best members are particularly assertive or confident, they are unlikely to promote themselves. They suffer from the same normative pressures as everyone else on the team and may withhold valuable information in the interest of *getting along*. Often, their information may never be revealed, or, frustratingly, it may be revealed at the end of a lengthy session—often when it's too late to be used. Leaders should remain sensitive to this possible problem and ensure that the best member is *called upon frequently* if they are reticent or unable to break into discussions dominated by others.

Collecting and displaying written input from all team members gathered before the meeting can short circuit this difficulty. It's also important to *draw out the introverts*. As we've discussed, some people analyze a problem best by thinking about it. Often extraverts will assume that silence means assent and rush on without taking full advantage of the insights and contributions that could be gleaned from the quiet members of the team. Team leaders should self-consciously ensure that introverts are invited to contribute regularly throughout the discussion.

The third dynamic of team discussion: team decisions tend to reflect the most socially desirable position. This is particularly true when that position seems *obviously true*. Again, the drive for *balance* and *harmony* is evident. Thus, the most socially desirable position is often the one that is held by the *majority*. The challenge is that this drive toward balance might produce a freight train effect that ignores valuable and highly pertinent information.

We know that in situations where the majority preference is known, opinions are public and no clear answer exists, teams typically will make the decision *initially preferred by the majority*. This tendency is exacerbated in situations in which individual team members are seeking *acceptance*. This might easily occur in settings in which a junior member of the organization is asked to serve on a team with senior management or where participation on the team is considered a genuine *perk*.

The unfortunate outcome of this dynamic is that the first idea proposed during a discussion carries disproportionate weight. The first idea suggested usually sets both the tone and direction of the discussion. If it seems obviously acceptable, it might also end the discussion because it will become the limit of the pool of common knowledge. As such, it will be discussed at greater length, repeated more frequently and remembered more by the team. This is an insidious dynamic because *teams routinely agree on the first plausible idea proposed* without recognizing that they are closing the door on other, potentially better, solutions. The attitude is "why make things harder than they have to be?"

The strategy for overcoming the problems associated with this dynamic is to simply *give all ideas equal weight with the first*. No matter how appealing it looks, teams must *resist the temptation to stop* with the first plausible suggestion. We know that this is a strong and seductive tendency. Teams can easily entertain a few ideas, but still give extra weight, time and attention to the first idea. Behind this movement is a drive for *conformity*. The more the team embraces an idea, the harder it will be for dissent to form. Instead, pressures will mount for agreement. It's probably wise, then, when list-building or recording team data, to *randomly* list ideas. Discussion leaders can monitor closely any premature discussion or "lobbying" for the first idea.

The fourth dynamic of active discussion: teams tend to make decisions that are more extreme, but in the same direction as individual preferences.

This is essentially a matter of *momentum*. Team discussion begins with some sense of dissonance created by the goal. Members know where they are and have some idea of where they would like to be. Discussion taps the expertise of various members and like a forward swinging pendulum, everyone's thinking advances. As the team moves toward consensus, momentum builds around their areas of agreement. Enthusiasm sets in as the goal is approached. Confidence grows as ideas are mutually reinforced.

In such circumstances, *teams will take greater risks than individual members will.* To some extent this reflects *"strength in numbers"* thinking and a weakening sense of individual accountability. The team is unstoppable! The opportunity reflected in this dynamic is that teams, by nature, will tend to *exceed the status quo.* They will push the limits (albeit tenderly) and go beyond where individuals could have been expected to go on their own. The challenge is that this momentum might propel a team *beyond* where it should go.

Whether it is in the direction of innovation or sticking to a failing course of action, a team's momentum can get it into trouble. A county health service conceived of a program dubbed *"House Calls."* The idea was to have a mobile health van with physicians and nurses visit patients in their home rather than in the clinic. The result was extremely poor utilization of physician and nurse services and a general decline in patient care countywide. Despite signs that the program was failing, the management team persisted with the implementation.

After the dust settled, no one on the team could be identified as the true program champion. Everyone had supported the decision, but no one had *personally* supported it with passion. It turned out that the team had basically been carried away with the potential and began to ignore all other signs of trouble. As individuals, none of the team members would have initiated the program or kept it going. As a team, however, it seemed like a great idea.

To avoid the problems associated with this dynamic, leaders should employ a strategy that *checks the appropriateness of the risk level before deciding.* Since teams tend to adopt positions that are more extreme than those advocated by individual members, particularly when the issue involves risk, care should be taken to assess the team's proposed action against a more *balanced* alternative. In general, *a team expecting a gain will be reluctant to assume risks* that while greatly increasing the potential profit equally increase the likelihood of simply breaking even. On the other hand, *when confronting a certain loss, teams are often willing to gamble.* They will assume a risk that promises equal chances of a large loss or breaking even rather than accept a certain, though modest loss.

Both views present problems. In the first situation, a conservative approach may support team *inertia* and *limit creativity.* This is why many companies fail to aggressively pursue new markets or products. In the second case, accepting high levels of risk may be unnecessary on a failing project. Again, inertia may lock a team into a project that should be abandoned and the losses cut. This is a common individual tendency whose impact is magnified by the team. Before finalizing a decision, teams should evaluate the level of risk being assumed and determine its appropriateness.

Managing Active Discussion

Team Dynamic	*Discussion Strategy*
Prefer common knowledge	- Accept all ideas - Critique each idea - Critically examine new data - Display all data
Under perform best member	- Identify best member - Foster participation
Conform to the popular position	- Give all ideas equal weight with first - Randomly list data for display
Take higher risks	- Check appropriateness of risk level - Assess against balanced approach

Avalanching

Avalanches are massive rock or snow slides. They are overwhelmingly powerful and have been clocked racing down mountainsides at over 90 miles per hour. Following an avalanche trails are tightly blocked. Anyone wishing to climb must dig through the rubble or crawl over it in order to continue. Teams endure avalanches as well.

Team avalanches are those behaviors that block the productivity of discussion. They are often subtle, but always powerful in their ability to impair or stop progress. Three common avalanching behaviors are *coasting, hiding and rehearsing.* They can appear individually or simultaneously during a discussion. Their pervasiveness makes them particularly insidious. Alone or together, they drain the vitality out of the discussion process and contribute to poor decisions and mediocre implementation.

Coasting refers to the tendency of teams to make *poor use of their time.* Unlike individuals, who tend to doggedly persist until their time limit is exhausted, teams *routinely fail to use all available time in completion of a task.* The sight of small groups at a seminar heading to the coffee bar ten minutes into a twenty-minute exercise is common.

This *coasting* comes in part from the sense that members will *not be held individually accountable* for the output and that team accountability is comfortably dispersed among the members. In essence, *no one* is accountable. Everyone feels safely anonymous. Coasting is also a factor when teams believe their *goal isn't really important* and doesn't warrant strenuous effort.

Coasting is easily overcome when teams have a *meaningful goal with a valued output,* when accountability is shared by *both* the team as a whole and each member, and when the allocated time is *appropriate* for the task.

Coasting as a team is closely related to *hiding* as an individual. *Hiding* is when a member decides to *let the others do the work.* The member is generally amenable to any team decision (easy agreement), but passive in the formulation of that decision. In such cases, these members believe that *their ideas aren't identifiable* in the team product and that *their ideas aren't valued.* Though the results are the same, the behavior has two distinct sources.

In the first instance, hiding may be prompted by boredom, disinterest in the task, distraction, resentment over the assignment, too much partying the night before, plain old laziness or a host of other reasons. The net result is that the member works for the team at a *reduced capacity* from what would be expected if working alone. Here again, issues of accountability come in to play.

Members who work at reduced rates believe that their contributions are not particularly noticeable in the final product. By doing enough to get along, they avoid criticism and conserve their energy for things they believe are important.

The only way to combat hiding is to make individuals *clearly accountable* for their participation. Labeling individual contributions in the minutes, actively drawing them into the discussion, assigning tasks such as recorder are all ways of keeping members from hiding. Having a *meaningful goal, assigning accountability* and *meeting only when necessary* are good ways to avoid the problems of hiding.

The second source of hiding is *fear of censure*. Hiding is often prevalent with members who lack confidence. They withhold comment because they believe the team will not respond well to their ideas. Teams that include prestigious or powerful members can easily *intimidate* less confident members. Also, teams that *tolerate sarcasm, blaming and ridicule* foster hiding. Hiding in this situation is usually manifested by quiet acquiescence.

As with the other avalanching behaviors, it is often impossible to tell if the member is silent because they have nothing to add, or silent because they fear speaking out. Many times hiding is noted only after the decision is made and in another setting the member brings up salient, valuable points that were missed by the team.

Hiding demonstrates why building member *confidence* before the task begins is so important. It also demonstrates the benefit of gathering input before the meeting when it will all be of *equal weight*. Networks, e-mail and the Web are tremendous equalizers in the area of idea generation and problem solving and can effectively counter hiding.

It's also very important that the team civics are in order. The fear of appearing foolish is a powerful regulator of adult conduct. Teams that create environments that are intolerant of critical, demeaning behavior will likely promote full participation by all members and greatly reduce incidents of hiding.

The final avalanching behavior is *rehearsing*. Almost everyone will at one time or another mentally rehearses his or her contribution to the discussion before speaking. Research has consistently shown that this period of rehearsing is the factor *chiefly responsible for productivity loss in idea generating and problem solving meetings*. When someone has a good idea in such a setting they are likely to lose it while waiting for an opportunity to speak. To counter this, they tend to mentally rehearse the idea. They mull it over, frame and reframe it, think about saying it out loud and may even anticipate possible objections.

Obviously, as they're doing this, they're *not generating additional ideas* and they are unable to *synergistically* build on the ideas of others. This behavior is made obvious when a member breaks in and asks to, "go back," to a point already discussed or makes a point, oblivious to the fact that the team is moved far ahead. Rehearsing is a vexing problem and difficult to correct. It can be minimized by *careful individual preparation* for the discussion and can be assisted by *detailed recording of information* during the discussion.

Station teams that permit the immediate recording of individual ideas should be used to the maximum extent possible. Often if appropriate questions are posed and answered prior to the face-to-face meeting much rehearsing is eliminated. Team leaders and facilitators should remain sensitive to this productivity block and watch for the non-verbal signs that someone has an idea to contribute. This presents yet another case in which member silence may actually be indicative of very active thought.

Controlling Avalanches

Productivity Blocker	*Management Strategy*
Coasting	- Set clear goals - Identify valued outputs - Share team/individual accountability - Give appropriate time to complete
Hiding	- Clear individual accountability - Give all input equal weight - Banish sarcasm, blaming, ridicule
Rehearsing	- Thorough pre-meeting preparation - Display data - Involve everyone

Second Thoughts

No team decision is truly final before it faces the court of *second thoughts*. *Second thoughts* are the recognition that just as members come to the meeting with a point of view, they will *leave* the meeting with a point of view. If you've implemented the techniques thus far, there's an excellent chance that members will leave with a firm commitment to the team decision. The only second thought that these members will have is satisfaction with a job well done. Unfortunately, we've already explored many ways that this commitment can be compromised. This is where WYSINWYG can turn cruel and the appearance of consensus can actually mask disagreement, disenfranchisement and even sabotage.

Second thoughts have their genesis in *first impressions*. It will come as no surprise that team members who adhered to a fixed belief before the discussion might well cling to their belief when the discussion is over. If the team decision doesn't support their point of view, they aren't likely to support it. Their lack of support, particularly if they broadcast it, may well doom the decision. In that case, these folks are usually ready to weigh in with a hearty "I told you so," or a more pointed, "I knew it wouldn't work."

When there are no "right" answers and persuasive arguments are used to make a case, *second thoughts* might occur among members who remained *unconvinced*. Often in the heat of discussion (or debate) a team member might be swayed, only to feel vaguely dissatisfied afterwards. The dissatisfaction might be because of new information gleaned from outsiders. It may also come from a sense of being *"sweet talked,"* or *"railroaded"* during the discussion. No matter what the reason, an unconvinced team member will be unable to effectively explain and defend the decision. In such situations, what started out as consensus will turn to tepid support and possibly further erode into non-support.

Team members whose first impressions were *flexible* can end up with second thoughts if they believe that *not all the alternatives were fully explored*. As with those who were unconvinced, these members might find new data to support another approach. This can easily happen when a member returns to their constituent group and tries to explain the decision. As others pose questions and the inevitable *"what ifs,"* the team member may begin to see new avenues for exploration.

It's also possible that these members might feel that a particular member or faction dominated the discussion. The result of the domination was that discussion was curtailed and not all options equally considered. Following the meeting (and safely away from the dominators) these members might begin to formulate new alternatives that seem equally as good as the team choice. Given a better alternative, their commitment to the original decision will fade rapidly.

Even members who approach the discussion with an attitude of *easy agreement* might develop second thoughts. Before the meeting they had some idea of the common attitudes of the team, but no particular personal commitment. In the course of the discussion they might have developed an attachment to a point of view that the team did not support. Similarly, following the meeting, when explaining the decision to others, this team member might realize that his *initial lack of commitment had been misguided.* He may discover that more was at stake than he originally believed and that the decision reached wasn't the best possible. Not only will this member come to regret his initial indifference, but also he'll be unlikely to support a choice that he now believes is wrong.

Finally, WYSINWYG teaches us that despite our best efforts, *things beyond our ability to recognize can derail teamwork.* The process of building and using station teams goes a long way toward ensuring excellent outcomes, but there are situations known only to the individual team members that might influence their support of the team decision. This is often the stuff of office politics. Sometimes it's a deeply personal issue. Ultimately each member is called upon to behave with integrity. Station teams create an environment in which every member can flourish. As long as this environment is nurtured, second thoughts from veiled sources will remain few and very far between.

Although second thoughts are virtually impossible to manage, there are *three strategies* that leaders can employ to gain a lock on commitment. The strategies can be employed in a meeting following the decision, or incorporated into the decision-making meeting itself. In either case, they provide an opportunity for the inclusion of information that may have been previously neglected and an evaluation of the team's initial assumptions as well.

The first strategy is to reflect before deciding. As active discussion clarifies the alternatives and advances toward a decision, it's possible to stop action and permit everyone to think through the problem again. The objective is to consider any data that may have bearing, but that has been *overlooked* or to address *lingering* questions. Again, this need not be a lengthy process, but the opportunity should be presented to identify any *outlying* information.

The pause before deciding should be *planned* into the project. While this can easily be done as a part of the decision-making meeting, it's often best to schedule it for a *follow-on meeting*. This gives everyone (and particularly the introverts) a chance to sort through the issues and either consolidate their support or raise some new questions. With this strategy, the original decision is considered provisional and confirmed at the follow-on meeting. There will be times that the decision must be made immediately. In these cases, teams can still build a period for reflection, or second thoughts into the agenda.

The second strategy requires the entire team to re-assess prior assumptions and decisions. While this rule is listed at the end of the decision-making process, it can be applied at *any* point. Simply stated, the team should feel free to revisit any previous assumptions and decisions to see if they are still valid. Further, they should feel free to *amend* them if necessary.

Filters on data that may have seemed appropriate at one time may no longer be necessary given new information. Restraints, barriers, deadlines, budgets, should all be regularly reviewed for appropriateness. Things do change and the team should be alert to events that might alter their focus. It is particularly helpful to do so before the final decision is reached as unnecessary or inappropriate previous decisions might well alter the final outcome.

This review isn't intended to upend the project moments before completion. It's simply a check to insure that with all the data brought to light, *the initial assumptions are still correct.* Better to amend the assumptions before reaching a final decision, than to have to begin again at a later date when someone else has noted a "changed" environment.

Finally, the third strategy is to provide a "last call" for reservations and dissent. This is the final opportunity for nagging concerns to be aired. If there are any, they should be displayed and thoroughly discussed. If a team member is uncertain at this point in the process, it's a clear sign that troubling second thoughts are in the team's future unless the concerns are completely addressed. This isn't the time to brush aside issues or pay lip service to dissent. Fully resolving issues at this point is the best insurance against silent disagreement that a team can buy.

Again, because teams tend to push for closure, it's important that time is *scheduled for this activity in advance.* A "last call" won't produce much input when it's presented at the end of a difficult work session in which exhaustion has long ago set. Station team techniques can be used at this point to ensure a full and fair hearing is given to all doubts. Providing this opportunity is a powerful sign that each team member has control over the final output. It promotes buy-in and creates an environment in which real consensus is likely.

Remember, to be effective, the team's decision must reflect the consensus of the group. Consensus depends upon *every* member believing that they have evaluated *all* pertinent data, have had constructive input during the discussion, and can now *accept* the final team decision. Achieving consensus may require compromise, but it should never accommodate surrender. Unless a member is certain that they can live with the decision, second thoughts will prevent them from supporting it during implementation.

To the Moon

We started this discussion by looking at a variety of decisions that put the first Americans on the moon. The Apollo program succeeded because thousands of men and women made consistently good decisions. From the visionary decision to go to the moon, to the exquisite hand-eye decisions on where to land, the program was characterized by the superb ability of the Apollo team to make the right choices. There were of course, missteps. The tragedy of Apollo 1 was undoubtedly the greatest. Yet even in disaster, the team resiliently pressed forward, learning from their errors and growing stronger.

All teams are ultimately evaluated on the strength of their decisions. Decision-making at the *Fifth Station* begins with what we *know* to be true about *decisions* and *teams*. It's predicated on what we *know* to be true about *confidence* and *motivation*. It reflects our *principles* and recognizes the profound *order* that underlies what we often see as chaotic.

Starting from the Fifth Station we're already *90% of the way* to achieving any goal and to achieving it with Apollo-like excellence. Beginning with our *decision-making style* and continuing through *first impressions, active discussion and second thoughts*, *Fifth Station* teams are ready to succeed. Every station team—your station team—is on the threshold of it's own lunar touchdown.

And Back Down to Earth

We started this journey at the base of Mt. Fuji. Of course, we didn't climb from the first station. We began at the fifth. That was the first lesson—the Fuji Rule—and it remains the most important. No matter what the task or challenge, always begin from your personal fifth station. Start with that foundation of experience. Build on your strengths and assets. Leverage what you're doing right to achieve the things you want, and success is certain.

Good luck on your climb!

SELECTED REFERENCES

Bandura, Albert and Daniel Cervone, " Self-Evaluative and Self-Efficacy Mechanisms Governing the Motivational Effects of Goal Systems," *Journal of Personality and Social Psychology*, Vol. 45, No. 5, 1983, 1017-1028.

Bandura, Albert and Robert Wood, "Effect of Perceived Controllability and Performance Standards on Self-Regulation of Complex Decision Making," *Journal of Personality and Social Psychology*, Vol. 56, No. 5, 1989, 805-814.

Bauer, Talya N. and Stephen G. Green, "Effect of Newcomer Involvement in Work-Related Activities: A Longitudinal Study of Socialization," *Journal of Applied Psychology*, Vol. 79, No. 2, 1994, 211-223.

Bouchard, Thomas J. Jr. and Melana Hare, "Size, Performance, and Potential in Brainstorming Groups," *Journal of Applied Psychology*, Vol. 54, No. 1, 1970, 51-55.

Buehler, Roger, Dale Griffin, and Michael Ross, "Exploring the 'Planning Fallacy:' Why People Underestimate Their Task-Completion Times," *Journal of Personality and Social Psychology*, Vol. 67, No. 3, 1994, 366-381.

Cialdini, Robert B. and Kenneth D. Richardson, "Two Indirect Tactics of Image Management: Basking and Blasting," *Journal of Personality and Social Psychology*, Vol. 39, No. 3, 1980, 406-415.

Csikszentmihalyi, Mihaly, *Flow: The Psychology of Optimal Experience*, New York, HarperCollins Publishers, 1990.

Day, David V. and Lorne M. Suisky, "Effects of Frame-of-Reference Training and Information Configuration on Memory Organization and Rating Accuracy,"
Journal of Applied Psychology, Vol. 80, No. 1, 1995, 158-167.

Dempster, Frank N., "The Spacing Effect: A Case Study in the Failure to Apply the Results of Psychological Research," *American Psychologist*, Vol. 43. No. 8, August 1988, 627-634.

Diehl, Michael and Wolfgang Stroebe, "Productivity Loss In Brainstorming Groups: Toward the Solution of a Riddle," *Journal of Personality and Social Psychology*, vol. 53, No. 3, 1987, 497-509.

Diehl, Michael and Wolfgang Stroebe, "Productivity Loss in Idea-Generating Groups: Tracking Down the Blocking Effect," *Journal of Personality and Social Psychology*, Vol. 61, No. 3, 1991, 392-403.

Earley, P. Christopher, Terry Connolly, and Göran Ekegren, "Goals, Strategy Development, and Task Performance: Some Limits on the Efficacy of Goal Setting," *Journal of Applied Psychology*, Vol. 74. No. 1, 1989,24-33.

Eden, Dov, "Pygmalion Without Interpersonal Contrast Effects: Whole Groups Gain From Raising Manager Expectations," *Journal of Applied Psychology*, Vol. 75, No. 4, 1990, 394-398.

Eden, Dov and Arle Aviram, "Self-Efficacy Training to Speed Reemployment: Helping People to Help Themselves," *Journal of Applied Psychology*, Vol. 78, No. 3, 1993, 352-360.

Eden, Dov and Joseph Kinnar, "Modeling Galatea: Boosting Self-Efficacy to Increase Volunteering," *Journal of Applied Psychology*, Vol. 76, No. 6, 1991, 770-780.

Elliot, Andrew J. and Patricia G. Devine, "On the Motivational Nature of Cognitive Dissonance: Dissonance as Psychological Discomfort," *Journal of Personality and Social Psychology*, Vol. 67, No. 3., 1994, 382-394.

Elliott, Elaine S. and Carol S. Dweck, "Goals: An Approach to Motivation and Achievement," *Journal of Personality and Social Psychology*, Vol. 54, No. 1, 1988, 5-12.

Fadiman, Clifton, Ed, *The Treasury of the Encyclopaedia Britannica*, New York, Viking Penguin, 1992.

Frankl, Victor E., *Man's Search for Meaning*, 3rd Ed., New York, Simon & Shuster, Inc., 1984.

Gallupe, R. Brent, Lana M. Bastianutti, and William H. Cooper, "Unblocking Brainstorms," *Journal of Applied Psychology*, Vol. 76, No. 1, 1991, 137-142.

Gardner, Howard, *Multiple Intelligences: The Theory in Practice*, New York, Basic Books, 1993.

Gilliland, Stephen W. and Donald S. Landis, "Quality and Quantity Goals in a Complex Decision Task: Strategies and Outcomes," *Journal of Applied Psychology*, Vol. 77, No. 5, 1992, 672-681.

Gist, Marilyn E., Catherine Schowerer and Benson Rosen, "Effects of Alternative Training Methods on Self-Efficacy and Performance in Computer Software Training," *Journal of Applied Psychology*, Vol. 74, No. 6, 1989, 884-891.

Glasser, William, *Control Theory*, New York, Harper and Row, 1984.

Gleick, James, *Chaos*, New York, Penguin Books, 1987.

Goleman, Daniel, *Emotional Intelligence*, New York, Bantam, 1995.

Hammer, Michael, and James Champy, *Reengineering the Corporation*, New York, Harper Business, 1993.

Harkins, Stephan G. and Kate Szymanski, "Social Loafing and Group Evaluation," *Journal of Personality and Social Psychology*, Vol. 56, No. 6, 1989, 934-941.

Hirsh, Sandra Krebs, and Jean M. Kummerow, *Introduction to Type in Organizations*, 2nd Ed., Palo Alto, Consulting Psychologists Press, Inc., 1990.

Kanfer, Ruth, Phillip L. Ackerman, Todd C. Murtha, Brad Dugdare, and Leissa Nelson, "Goal Setting, Conditions of Practice, and Task Performance: A Resource Allocation Perspective," *Journal Of Applied Psychology*, Vol. 79. No. 6, 1994,826-835.

Kaufman, Gary M. and Terry A. Beehr, "Interactions Between Job Stressors and Social Support; Some Counterintuitive Results," *Journal of Applied Psychology*, Vol. 71, No. 3, 1986, 522-526.

Kraiger, Kurt, J. Kevin Ford, and Eduardo Salas, "Application of Cognitive, Skill-Based, and Affective Theories of Learning Outcomes to New Methods of Training Evaluation," *Journal of Applied Psychology*, Vol. 78, No. 2, 1993, 311-328.

Kroeger, Otto, and Janet M. Thuesen, *Type Talk*, New York, Dell Publishing, 1988.

Kroeger, Otto, with Janet M. Thuesen, *Type Talk at Work*, New York, Dell Publishing, 1992.

Kuhn, Thomas S., *The Structure of Scientific Revolutions*, 3rd Ed., Chicago, University of Chicago Press, 1996.

Langston, Christopher A., "Capitalizing On and Coping With Daily-Life Events: Expressive Responses to Positive Events," *Journal of Personality and Social Psychology*, Vol. 67, No. 6., 1994, 1112-1125.

Larson, James R., Jr., Pennie G. Foster-Fishman, and Christopher B. Keys, "Discussion of Shared and Unshared Information in Decision-Making Groups," *Journal of Personality and Social Psychology*, Vol. 67, No. 3, 1994, 448-481.

Martocchio, Joseph J., "Effects of Conceptions of Ability on Anxiety, Self-Efficacy, and Learning in Training," *Journal of Applied Psychology*, Vol. 79, No. 6, 1994, 819-825.

Maslow, A. H., *Religions, Values, and Peak-Experiences*, New York, Penguin, 1994.

McGuire, Timothy W., Sara Kiesler, and Jane Siegel, "Group and Computer-Mediated Discussion Effects in Risk Decision Making," *Journal of Personality and Social Science*, Vol. 52, No. 5, 1987, 917-930.

McNeely, Bonnie L. and Bruce M. Meglino, "The Role of Dispositional and Situational Antecedents in Prosocial Organizational Behavior: An Examination of the Intended Beneficiaries of Prosocial Behavior," *Journal of Applied Psychology*, Vol. 79, No. 6, 1994, 836-844.

Meyers, Isabel Briggs, *Introduction to Type*, 5th Ed., Palo Alto, Consulting Psychologists Press, Inc., 1993.

Myers, Isabel Briggs, and Mary H. McCaully, *Manual: A Guide to the Development and Use of the Meyers-Briggs Type Indicator*, Palo Alto, Consulting Psychologists Press, Inc., 1985.

Myers, Katherine D., and Linda K. Kirby, *Introduction to Type: Dynamics and Development*, Palo Alto, Consulting Psychologists Press, Inc., 1994

Peale, Norman Vincent, *The Power of Positive Thinking*, New York, Prentice-Hall Inc., 1992.

Riggs, Matt L. and Patrick A. Knight, "The Impact of Perceived Group Success-Failure on Motivational Beliefs and Attitudes: A Causal Model," *Journal of Applied Psychology*, Vol. 79, No. 5, 1994, 755-766.

Roberts, Karlene H. and Charles A. O'Reilly III, "Relationships Among Components of Credibility and Communication Behaviors in Work Units," *Journal of Applied Psychology*, Vol. 61. No. 1, 1975, 99-102.

Rogelberg, Steven G., Janet L. Barnes-Farrell, and Charles A. Lowe, "Stepladder Technique: An Alternative Group Structure Facilitating Effective Group Decision Making," *Journal of Applied Psychology*, Vol. 77, No. 5, 1992, 730-737.

Rosenthal, R., and L. Jacobson, *Pygmalion in the Classroom: Teacher expectations and pupil's intellectual development,* New York, Holt, Rinehart & Winston, 1968.

Scher, Steven J. and Joel Cooper, "Motivational Basis of Dissonance: The Singular Role of Behavioral Consequences," *Journal of Personality and Social Psychology,* Vol. 56, No. 6, 1989, 899-906.

Seligman, Martin E. P., *Learned Optimism,* New York, Pocket Books, 1990.

Shore, Lynn McFarlane and Sandy J. Wayne, "Commitment and Employee Behavior: Comparison of Affective Commitment and Continuance Commitment With Perceived Organizational Support," *Journal of Applied Psychology,* Vol. 78, No 5, 1993, 774-780.

Shepard, Alan, and Deke Slayton, *Moon Shot,* Atlanta, Turner Publishing Inc., 1994.

Simonson, Itamar and Barry M. Staw, "Deescalation Strategies: A Comparison of Techniques for Reducing Commitment to Losing Courses of Action," *Journal of Applied Psychology,* Vol. 77, No. 4, 1992, 419-426.

Sproull, Lee, and Sara Kiesler, *Connections: New Ways of Working in the Networked Organization,* Cambridge, MIT Press, 1993.

Straus, Susan G. and Joseph E. McGrath, "Does the Medium Matter? The Interaction of Task Type and Technology on Group Performance and Member Reactions," *Journal of Applied Psychology,* Vol. 79. No. 1, 1994, 87-97.

Tetlock, Philip E., "A Value Pluralism Model of Ideological Reasoning," *Journal of Personality and Social Psychology*, Vol. 50, No. 4, 1986, 819-827.

Tetlock, Philip E. and Richard Boettger, "Accountability: A Social Magnifier of the Dilution Effect," *Journal of Personality and Social Psychology*, Vol. 57, No. 3, 1989, 389-398.

Tetlock, Philip E., Linda Skitka and Richard Boettger, "Social and Cognitive Strategies for Coping With Accountability: Conformity, Complexity, and Bolstering," *Journal of Personality and Social Psychology*, Vol. 57, No. 4, 1989, 632-640.

Thomas, Kecia M. and John E. Mathieu, "Role of Causal Attributions in Dynamic Self-Regulation and Goal Processes," *Journal of Applied Psychology*, Vol. 79, No. 6, 1994, 812-818.

Weingart, Laurie P., "Impact- of Group Goals, Task Component Complexity, Effort, and Planning on Group Performance," *Journal of Applied Psychology*, Vol. 77, No. 5, 1992, 652-693.

Wolin, Steven J., and Sybil Wolin, *The Resilient Self: How Survivors of Troubled Families Rise Above Adversity*, New York, Villard Books, 1993.

Wood, Robert and Albert Bandura, "Impact of Conceptions of Ability on Self-Regulatory Mechanisms and Complex Decision Making," *Journal of Personality and Social Psychology*, Vol. 56, No. 3, 1989, 407-415.